HAUNTED
YORK

The author, Rupert Matthews.

HAUNTED
YORK

RUPERT MATTHEWS

The
History
Press

First published 2009

The History Press
The Mill, Brimscombe Port
Stroud, Gloucestershire, GL5 2QG
www.thehistorypress.co.uk

© Rupert Matthews, 2009

The right of Rupert Matthews to be identified as the Author
of this work has been asserted in accordance with the
Copyrights, Designs and Patents Act 1988.

ISBN 978 0 7524 4910 4

Typesetting and origination by The History Press
Printed in Great Britain

CONTENTS

Introduction   7

Tour of Haunted York   9

INTRODUCTION

The ancient city of York is one of the most magnificent cities in England. It is also one of the most haunted.

Nobody is entirely certain how many ghosts lurk among the ancient walls of York; there are certainly dozens of them, maybe over a hundred. Some ghosts stalk the streets and chambers of the city with alarming frequency, others appear only once or twice a year and a few appear so infrequently that some researchers believe they may have left this mortal world for good. The ghosts come in a bewildering variety of shapes and sizes. There are ancient ghosts, modern ghosts, male ghosts, female ghosts and ghosts so elusive that nobody knows anything very much about them at all.

But be they Roman soldiers, a Tudor gentleman, Grey Lady or enigmatic footsteps in empty rooms, these ghosts all have one thing in common: the city of York itself. It is a city with a character all of its own, moulded and shaped over more than 2,000 years of history.

There was some sort of a settlement here in Celtic times, but York enters history in AD 71 when the Romans built a fortress here and named it *Eboracum*. Over the years the name has shifted and altered, but it remains rooted in that first designation. The modern name of York is derived from the 'orac' element of the Roman name, coming to us by way of the Viking *Jorvik*.

Amazingly there are still remnants of Roman *Eboracum* to be seen. The western corner of the fortress was protected by a massive, multi-angular buttress which still stands in Museum Street, while the museum itself contains fine statues, coins and other remains. There are even Roman ghosts still tramping through the city as their human counterparts once did in life – we shall come to their haunts almost as soon as we enter the city.

On the whole, however, York is a medieval city. It is dominated by the vast York Minster at one end of the city and the powerful Clifford's Tower at the other. When the Norman conqueror, King William I, came here in 1069 he casually burned down the Anglo-Viking city that had defied his right to rule. Then he ordered the construction of a circuit of walls that surrounded 263 acres of land. The walls seen today date mostly from later centuries, but they stand on the foundations laid by William.

The Normans also built a minster, but it was torn down in 1220 and the construction of the present church begun. Work went on for 250 years to produce the magnificent mass of masonry that today dominates the city centre, and which contains one of Europe's finest collections of medieval stained glass. We shall meet that glass again for it is linked to one of York's phantoms. While the cathedral was being constructed, other teams of workmen were erecting the forbidding fortress of Clifford's Tower at the southern end of the medieval city. That too has its spectres that we shall meet in this book.

The most pervasive remnant of the Middle Ages to survive in York is less tangible, but far more influential. The street layout of the city took its present form during this period, picking up names from Viking, English and Norman eras as well as more recent periods. The streets are usually thronged with tourists, and always with locals, but there remains space among them for the ghosts and phantoms who like to wander their old haunts.

Though the street layout remains from medieval times, most of the old houses and shops vanished long ago, to be replaced by imposing Georgian residences. When Victoria came to the throne, she brought with her railways and a booming industrialisation that both left their mark on the city. So important was the rail industry to York, and vice versa, that the National Rail Museum is now located here, while old factories and workshops in various stages of decay and renovation abound.

Through all these ages, the city of York has endured. It has been burned to the ground more than once, ravaged by invading armies and yet always it has managed to rise again to greater glories. No less enduring are the ghosts that throng its walls and streets.

It is perhaps best to start a tour of ghostly York with the oldest and most famous of all the ghosts that lurk in this ancient city.

Rupert Matthews, 2009

TOUR OF HAUNTED YORK

A Roman in the Cellar of the Treasurer's House

The Treasurer's House takes its name from its earlier use as the home and office complex belonging to the Treasurer of York Minster. It is appropriate, therefore, that it lies in the shadow of the Minster. The house stands in Minster Yard at the northern end of College Street, just east of the Minster. It is now owned by the National Trust and is open most days of the year.

In the thirteenth century, when the house was first built, the Minster was a monastery owning vast estates as well as being the mother church for all of northern England. Vast sums of money poured in from the farms, mills and weirs that the Minster owned, then flowed out again to give relief to the poor, educate churchmen and as tribute to Rome. The Treasurer's House was a hive of activity as teams of monks, clerks and support staff pored over the accounts, counted the money and kept meticulous records. The house has been much altered since those days, and today almost nothing of the medieval structure can be seen above ground. Below ground level, however, the thirteenth-century house is almost intact. The foundations and cellars are pretty much as they were when the monks worked there. And it is in the cellars that the ghosts lurk.

Among those who lived or worked in the Treasurer's House, the cellars had always had something of an odd reputation. Nobody was ever willing to talk to outsiders about what went on down there, but many people knew that it was not a place to linger alone. One person who did not know this was a young apprentice plumber by the name of Harry Martindale. It was 1953 and the Treasurer's House was having modern central heating installed. Harry was tasked with checking over the joints of pipes installed by his more experienced colleagues, which was why he went down into the cellar – alone.

Harry was intent on his work when the incident began. He was up a short ladder so that he could check piping that was running along just below the cellar ceiling. He heard a muffled trumpet blast, but took no notice. He thought perhaps a band was practising nearby. The trumpet came again, nearer this time. Again Harry ignored it. Then a horse stepped out of the solid wall right in front of Harry's eyes. Thunderstruck and terrified in equal measure, Harry

The Treasurer's House is open to the public and was the scene of one of the classic and best documented ghost sightings in York.

fell off his ladder and tumbled to the floor. As he scrambled to get away from the figure of the horse, Harry could not tear his eyes from the apparition.

The horse continued to emerge from the wall into the cellar. On its back was a man in a long cloak and a helmet with a feather crest on it. Behind the horseman came a dozen or more men on foot. As Harry gradually recovered from his shock, he was deeply relieved to see that the ghosts paid him not the slightest bit of attention but marched on as if he were not there. The men on foot carried large, round shields with long spears slung over their shoulders and short swords hanging from their belts. They had what looked like kilts, dyed a dark green colour, and mail shirts. One of them carried a trumpet that was long, straight and battered as if from long years of hard use.

As the men marched across the cellar, Harry realised that he could not see them from the knees downward. Then the horsemen came to a spot where a hole had been dug into the floor. Harry could now see the horse's legs almost down to the hooves. They carried shaggy hair around the fetlocks, similar to those on a modern shire horse. As the men on foot passed the hole, Harry could see their legs down to the ankles. They were wearing leather sandals attached by straps that ran criss-cross fashion up to the knees. The men marched on, giving out an aura of dejection and despondency, until they vanished into the wall opposite.

As soon as they were gone, Harry leaped to his feet and bolted up the stairs to the ground floor. Running desperately to find his foreman, Harry bumped into the curator of the museum that occupies the house. The curator took one look at Harry's pale face and said, 'Oh. You've seen

The descriptions given of the ghostly soldiers seen in the cellar of the Treasurer's House match those of the later Roman Imperial Army of about AD 350. The figure shown here is typical of the period.

the Romans then.' He took Harry aside, calmed him down and then asked him to dictate a detailed description of what he had seen. The curator then showed Harry other accounts of the ghosts in the cellar.

Most of these other reports match the experience of young Harry Martindale almost precisely. One that is slightly different was recounted by a young lady attending a fancy dress party back in the days when the house was a private residence. During the party the guests were given time to explore the house. The lady chose to venture down the stairs to the cellar. She went to enter one of the various rooms, but suddenly a man stepped out from the shadows to bar the open doorway. He was dressed in a mail shirt and had on his head a plumed helmet, just like those seen by Harry and others. The figure said nothing, but glared at the girl and held his spear out to make it clear that she was not welcome. After hesitating for a few seconds, the woman retreated back up the stairs. She asked her host who the curmudgeonly guest in Roman armour might be, but there was no guest wearing Roman armour. The incident is usually put down as a sighting of the ghosts, though on this occasion the spectre did not behave as usual.

The description of the figures given by Harry was rather more detailed than those recounted by other witnesses and has led to some detailed investigations. Excavations have shown that a Roman road runs underneath the Treasurer's House, leading from what had been a gate in the fortress walls to the east toward the headquarters building that stood where the Minster nave is now. The ghosts follow the route of this former road precisely. Even more interestingly, the surface of the road is about eighteen inches below the cellar floor, and some three inches lower than the bottom of the hole that was there in Harry's day. The ghosts are, of course, seen only from the knees up so it would seem that they are marching along the surface of the old road that existed when they were alive.

The description given by Harry of men in mail shirts with round shields does not match that of Roman soldiers shown in most books. However, the armour thought of as typical for Romans, with large oblong shields and armour made up of strips of metal, was used only by the legionaries who formed the backbone of the Roman army. Rather more numerous were the auxiliaries recruited from tribes within the Empire and, in later times, the mercenaries recruited from tribes outside the Empire.

The description given by Harry matches most closely auxiliaries of the later third or fourth centuries. This was a time when the Roman Empire was in decline with a collapsing economy and decreasing population. The climate had been rather warmer than it is today for around 300 years. However, it was now cooling, making it more difficult to grow crops, especially in Britain. And the barbarians were becoming bolder and more aggressive. The collapse of Roman power in Britain was not far off. No wonder the ghosts seem so dejected.

The Romans are not the only ghosts to lurk in the Treasurer's House. In January 1674 it was the town house of the Aislaby family of Fountains Hall. Staying with them was a Miss Mary Maillorie, a relative who was engaged to marry Mr Jonathan Jennings of York. On 10 January the Aislabys and the young Mary went to attend a ball given by the Duke of Buckingham – we shall be meeting him again later – at which Jonathan was also present. Unsurprisingly, Mary spent most of the evening with Jonathan. When the Aislabys decided to go home, they could find young Mary nowhere. They left a burly servant with a lantern to search for her and escort her home through the dark streets, then went home to bed.

According to Mary's account given when she turned up at the Treasurer's House next morning, she had missed the servant and been escorted home by Jonathan and his manservant. When they had arrived, the house was dark and silent. Nobody answered their knocks. Jonathan and his man had then led Mary to the home of his female relative where she spent the night. George Aislaby, the head of the family, suspected the worst and despite the fact that the servant and relative backed up Mary's account, he challenged Jonathan Jennings to a duel to restore the young woman's honour.

The fight took place on the fields that then stretched out from Bootham Bar. It was a brief affair that ended with George Aislaby being wounded. The injury did not seem serious, and the man was helped home by his second while Jennings likewise went home. Unfortunately the wound got infected and George Aislaby died. Realising that he might be in danger of prosecution for murder, Aislaby hurried to see the Duke of Buckingham. The nobleman lent Jennings a coach and wrote him a letter of introduction and explanation to King Charles II. Jennings hurried off to court where he explained the affair and received a royal pardon for the death.

Meanwhile, George Aislaby was laid out in the room where he died, then carried to the Minster for burial. His ghost remains in the house, being seen from time to time standing quietly in a downstairs room. He is generally not seen for very long, fading from view almost as soon as he is noticed.

The Ghost Child at No. 5 College Street

After visiting the Treasurer's House, leave by way of the main entrance, bear right through Minster Yard and then bear left into College Street. Look for house No. 5. This house is a private residence and is not open to the public. But the ghost is well known because the family that lived there in the 1930s were not only happy to talk about it in public, but called in a medium to investigate.

The haunting began when the parents thought that they heard one of their children calling out from their upstairs bedrooms, but when they went up, they found the children all peacefully asleep. This happened several times and much puzzled the parents. Then one of the children mentioned hearing the sounds of another child crying, while a second child said that she had sometimes seen a little girl skipping about upstairs.

Convinced that they were dealing with a ghostly child, the parents called in a medium to investigate. The psychic claimed to make contact with the little girl, who was aged seven at the time of her death. The medium passed on a heart-rending story from the spirit of the girl. Back in the seventeenth century, plague had hit York. One of the adults at No. 5 College Street, had contracted the disease and the house was put into quarantine. Over the next few days the awful disease worked its way through the family, killing all but the little girl. Alone and afraid in the house of the dead, she had retreated to her bedroom upstairs where she had herself died, though whether from the plague or starvation was unclear.

Investigators tried to check out the story. York had certainly suffered visitations of the plague more than once in the seventeenth century. It was certainly the practice of the City Council to impose quarantine on any house where a person fell sick with the plague. The usual routine was for a red cross and the words 'Lord have mercy on our souls' to be painted on the front door, which was then locked and barricaded from the outside. Guards were posted both to stop persons from entering or leaving the affected house and to pass in food and water to those incarcerated within. Sadly records have not survived detailing who lived at No. 5 College Street during the plague years, so it is impossible to show whether or not the story passed on by the medium was true.

Murder, Betrayal and Suicide at St William's College

Also in College Street is St William's College after which the road is named. The first ghost here is a gentle, friendly soul. She takes the form of an elderly lady wearing a long dress with apron and shawl who sits on the front step as if waiting for a friend to come by. She smiles and nods at passers-by. Unfortunately nobody knows who she is, when she lived nor for whom she has been waiting all these decades.

St William's College was built to be a residence for priests serving the various chantry chapels in the Minster. One of the ghosts dates back to this early period.

The other ghost here has a history almost as tragic – albeit entirely self-inflicted – as that of the little girl at No. 5. In the days of Henry VIII in the early sixteenth century, before the Reformation swept away the Minster monastery, the college provided rooms to clergy and clerks working at the nearby religious house. For some reason that has never been properly explained, one of these clerks incurred the wrath of two local brothers. The men decided to murder the clerk.

They laid in wait for their victim to return to his rooms on the upper floor of the college late one evening. The unfortunate man stood no chance against the cowardly assault, was taken entirely by surprise and dispatched in seconds. The brothers then ransacked the rooms for anything valuable and fled. The murder was soon discovered, of course, and the authorities began their investigations. For some reason the younger brother feared that he was under suspicion and went to his brother. The elder brother advised him to hide in a wooden chest, promising to bring him regular supplies of food and drink until he could discover if the man was really under suspicion or not.

Instead, the treacherous elder brother went straight to the local magistrates. He took with him some of the items stolen from the murdered man's rooms and said that he had found them in his younger brother's possession. The magistrates swallowed the story that it was the younger brother who was alone guilty of the killing. The elder brother told the magistrates where the man might be found and officials were dispatched to find him. The man was arrested, his room searched and more incriminating evidence found. He was quickly found guilty and hanged.

The elder brother who had saved his neck by sending his own brother to the scaffold was unable to find any rest. Remorse and guilt soon became his constant companions. Time and again he returned to the scene of the crime, pacing up and down while wringing his hands and muttering under his breath. He died a few weeks later, though whether by suicide or some more natural cause was not recorded.

To this day the upper chamber where the crime took place is haunted by the sound of pacing footsteps. Traditionally the footsteps are said to belong to the remorseful elder brother, but since the phantom has never been seen this must remain uncertain. It is just as likely to be the murder victim.

Direct from God: Madness at York Minster

Having passed St William's College, continue along College Street to its southern end. Then turn right into Deangate, keeping the soaring mass of Gothic architecture that is York Minster to your right. The public entrance to this fine and ancient church is through the West Front, so pass along Deangate to its far end, then bear right to enter the Minster.

There are several ghosts here, but perhaps the most endearing was seen only once. In 1964 a team of stonemasons was at work on the West Front. The elements have not always been kind to the Minster, so the exterior stonework needs to be replaced, re-pointed and generally cared for from time to time. A woman visitor to York stopped to watch the stonemasons at work. She noticed a particularly intricately carved piece of medieval stonework that was being renovated. Just then, a workman came ambling up to stand beside her. He too stopped to stare at the stonework. The woman glanced at the man, noticing that he was squat and scruffily dressed, with a cloth cap or hat of some kind on his head. The workman smiled. 'I carved that.' he said. 'Do you like it?'

Before the woman could answer, the workman vanished into thin air. It gave her quite a fright, but on reflection she decided that the figure had been the ghost of the anonymous mason who had carved the piece some 600 years earlier, come back to make sure that the modern stonemasons were up to his standards.

Other phantoms lurk within the Minster. Of these, the best known is Dean Gale. The good dean was head of the Minster chapter in the late seventeenth century, winning the admiration and respect of the citizens of York for his tireless and assiduous devotion to his duties. He attended nearly every service that was held in the Minster during his time, always occupying the same seat in the choir. Dean Gale died in 1702, much mourned by all who knew him, and was buried in the Minster that he loved so much. His tomb can still be seen.

The work of the Minster went on, of course, with the usual round of religious services and a new dean was soon found. About six weeks after Dean Gale passed away, a Mr Hawley was invited to read the second lesson at a service of Holy Communion. Mr Hawley climbed up into the pulpit and read his piece. But instead of then descending and returning to his seat, the man stood silent and still as if rooted to the spot. When a nearby clergyman gently tugged his coat, Mr Hawley seemed suddenly to come to. He stumbled down from the pulpit

The Minster seen from the north. The ghosts that inhabit the building are a mixed lot.

and walked back to his seat. When asked what had caused his sudden immobility, Mr Hawley said that on finishing his reading he had happened to glance at the seats in the choir and had been astonished to see the wraith of the recently deceased Dean Gale sitting in his usual seat. Thereafter several of those chosen to read a lesson have seen the ghost of the genial old dean sat in his usual place.

A rather more anonymous ghost was seen in the Minster in the 1840s. The names of those involved were kept secret when the story came out in a local magazine and today nobody knows the names of either the witnesses or the ghost. It is worth recounting, however, as it is typical of a class of phantoms known to researchers as 'crisis apparitions'.

On the day in question a local York man, identified by only the initials B.L., was showing some visiting friends around the Minster. At one point B.L. was in the nave with a young lady, whose father and mother had wandered off to look at some tombs of interest. As B.L. and the girl

The West Front of York Minster, where the replacement of some worn medieval stonework led to the appearance of a phantom stonemason.

were strolling toward the crossing, a man in full naval uniform started walking toward them. B.L. thought it odd that an officer should be in uniform when presumably off duty and was about to point the man out to his companion when he realised that the girl had stopped dead and was staring at the approaching man.

B.L. was alarmed to see the young woman's face turn pale and her eyes widen as if in shock. The naval officer was by this point only a yard or two in front of them. He stopped, looked at the young woman with what B.L. thought was a familiarity and touching kindness and then said, 'There is a future state.' At this the girl tottered backward and collapsed on to a pew. B.L. dashed to sit beside her, thinking that she had fainted or been taken ill. When he looked around for the naval officer who had provoked such a strong reaction, there was no sign of him.

After a few minutes the young lady recovered her composure. She asked B.L. not to mention the incident to her mother and father, promising to explain later. That evening, she told

B.L. that the man they had seen in the Minster was her brother, a naval officer who at that very moment was on duty with his ship thousands of miles away. Apparently the brother and sister had promised each other that if either of them should die, they would make every effort to visit the other to tell them what happened to the soul after death. The girl was convinced that her brother had died, and that he had appeared to her as a ghost to announce that there was an afterlife.

B.L. was at the time unconvinced, but a few days later a message arrived from the navy announcing the accidental death of the brother. It had occurred on the day that his spectre had appeared in the Minster.

These 'crisis apparitions' are among the most common types of ghost. Generally they appear only once but when they do manifest themselves they do so very clearly and appear to be perfectly solid and real to the people that see them. As in the case of this naval officer, most crisis apparitions appear at about the time the person dies, and are seen by a close relative or loved one. Interestingly, however, a few such phantoms have been seen not when a person dies, but when they are involved in a life-threatening incident such as a car crash, heart attack or battle. These are among the few times that the ghost of a living person is to be encountered.

Rather more likely to be seen by visitors to the Minster are those phantoms that, unlike the naval officer, return time and again. The most firmly identified is the phantom of a most unfortunate man by the name of Jonathan Martin. Martin was born into a respectable and reasonably wealthy family at Haydon Bridge in 1783. As a young man he joined the navy, serving with distinction against the French and receiving a wound to the head that his family blamed for what followed.

After the war ended in 1815, Martin returned to Yorkshire, got married and seemed to settle down. However, he soon began to show signs of being obsessed with religion, believing himself to be an instrument of God's will and expressing deep contempt for established religion. After he threatened to shoot the Bishop of Oxford, his family had him inspected by doctors who advised that he should be confined for his own safety, and that of others. By 1828 he seemed to have recovered somewhat, and was allowed by his family to live in rooms in York.

Martin had, however, merely masked his madness to escape confinement. He began writing anonymous letters to clergymen condemning them as the Devil's servants and making horrific threats against them. By January 1829 he had become bolder, signing the letters with his initials of J.M.

On 1 February Martin went to the Minster and hid himself in a quiet corner until after the public had been ushered out at twilight and the great doors locked shut. He then came out of hiding and stripped himself naked – the better for carrying out God's will, according to him. He then used a razor to strip cloth from the fixtures, and a hammer to smash up wooden furniture. This he piled up in the choir and set on fire. The flames spread gradually, he said, but by the early hours of the morning the blaze was well established. He smashed a window and fled back to his rooms.

The fire was discovered by choristers arriving at 6 a.m. for morning service. By then the fire had got into the roof of the choir and was both well established and running wild. The city fire brigade was called, but it took all day to get the fire under control and it was not out until the following day. The choir had been gutted and other parts of the Minster badly damaged. It took years to repair.

It took only a few days, however, for the magistrates to link the threatening letters signed 'J.M.' to the fire and then to Jonathan Martin, lately released from confinement for mental illness. Martin was arrested on 8 February and his trial began on 31 March. Martin's family hired a top-class lawyer for the defence, but the effort was doomed to failure when the accused not only agreed with almost everything the prosecution lawyer said, but gleefully added details of his own. He declared that he had acted on instructions direct from God and that his actions had cleansed the city of sin. There was no doubt that he was guilty, the only question that the jury had to decide was whether he was sane, in which case he would hang, or whether he was mad, in which case he would be confined in a public mental asylum.

In the event the jury took only seven minutes to declare that Martin was mad. He was sent to an asylum. He died in 1838 without ever losing his belief that he alone was the instrument of God's will on Earth. His ghost promptly returned to the choir of York Minster, the scene of his greatest work. To the profound embarrassment of most of those who see his phantom, the ghost prances around as stark naked as he was on the night that he set minster on fire.

After the fire, the Minster authorities hired a team of nightwatchmen who took it in turns to stay overnight in the great church. These men got used to hearing assorted odd sounds as the air moved around the church and the roof cooled and contracted after absorbing heat from the summer sun. But there was one thing that they saw which none could explain: a pillar of blue light around six feet tall and two feet in diameter would sometimes manifest itself at the western end of the nave. Sometimes it remained still for some minutes before fading away, at other times it would drift slowly across the nave toward the crossing before flickering and vanishing from view. The pillar of light never made a sound. One nightwatchman, Mr Gladin, encountered the blue light when he had his dog with him. The dog instantly bolted and would never again enter the church.

Rather more gentle is the ghostly man who walks the nave. This gentleman wears hose and doublet that would seem to date his days as a mortal to the reign of Elizabeth I. Who he is and why he haunts the Minster is not known. He simply strolls quietly along ignoring those around him.

A pair of equally serene ghosts have been seen in the north transept, close to the window dedicated to the nurses who worked to alleviate the suffering of wounded soldiers during the First World War. They are the phantoms of two young women, though whether they were nurses is unclear.

'Odd feelings' in Room 36, Dean Court Hotel

Leaving the Minster, you will find yourself facing the Dean Court Hotel, which has two ghost tales attached to it. The first is something of a puzzle. The less active phantom is often described as being that of a Roman soldier in eyewitness accounts. However, this is odd as Roman soldiers have not marched in York for some 1,600 years while the Dean Court was constructed in around 1850 as lodgings for visiting clergy.

It seems to be the ghost's helmet that has led to him being identified as a Roman, and yet he is not always seen very clearly and some descriptions of the spectre could be interpreted as being that of almost any man wearing a metal helmet. If it were seen only on the ground

The Dean Court Hotel has three ghosts lurking within its walls, though one of them may not be quite what it appears to be.

floor, one might argue that this Roman ghost was walking on the ground level as it existed in Roman times and was ignoring the construction of a building that was not there in his day. After all, this site does lie within the area covered by the old legionary fortress that was the start of the city of York. The army headquarters stood just east of here, so it would be an area where soldiers came and went with frequency.

However, the ghost is seen upstairs as well as downstairs, so that explanation cannot be the true one. He must, presumably, be the phantom of somebody who passed this way since the hotel was built. But who he was and why he returns in a stout military helmet, nobody knows.

The other, and in recent years considerably more active, phantom is to be found in the cellar. This is the ghost of a cleaner woman who dates back to the Victorian era. The cleaner worked here when the cellar was shared with a next-door property that was named Vollans. It is assumed that the cleaner stored her tools in the cellar, or perhaps she had rooms there, which might account for her fondness for the place.

One night in 2008 the Dean Court Hotel played host to a 'ghost watch' by a local group of paranormal investigators. Although the management took great care not to let slip any details of the supposed hauntings, two different investigators reported seeing a cleaning woman of the Victorian era. One said that she sensed the word 'vollans' or something similar – which was spot on.

An early twentieth-century photograph of the annex to the Dean Court Hotel, then a separate structure called Vollans. The ghostly maid dates back to this time.

The third paranormal visitor to the Dean Court is invisible. There have been some odd 'feelings' in Room 36. These take the form of a pressure being felt pushing down on the bed and a frequently reported cold spot, even on warm days.

This is not enough to put off visitors, and with reason. The Dean Court has a great restaurant which has won two AA Rosettes, and in 2008 won the Yorkshire Tourist Board's prestigious White Rose Award as Hotel of the Year.

A Manifestation in the Gentlemen's Toilet: Poltergeists at the York Arms

Leaving the Dean Court, turn left and then turn left again to pass along the side wall of the hotel into the thoroughfare of Petergate. The York Arms pub is at No. 26 on your right.

The York Arms pub looks out toward the Dean Court Hotel. The phantom lady here is one of the most active in York.

This particular pub has a ghostly lady who rarely gives any trouble. She is seen for the most part standing on or near the staircase. She wears a long dress of a pale colour, though whether it is a pale blue or pale green depends on which witness you talk to. The apparition remains in sight for a second or two, then fades away. The only time this phantom caused any real alarm came one evening in the 1970s when she manifested herself in the gentlemen's toilet just as one customer was about to relieve himself. It quite put him off, apparently.

Despite the fact that she is generally reckoned to be no trouble, the lady of the York Arms has sometimes been linked to the poltergeist manifestations that struck the property in the 1980s. In this case, the poltergeist was a fairly persistent entity, but one given only to the milder forms of activity associated with such supernatural visitors. The phantom opened doors that had been left shut and shut those that were left open. It moved glasses about the bar, hid kitchen utensils and was forever rearranging the cutlery drawer.

Unlike most ghosts, poltergeists are never seen. They are identified only by the things that they do. These will often begin with knockings, scratches and rappings, which may be mistaken for the sounds of mice or naughty children. The haunting then progresses to the sorts of antics encountered in the York Arms. Objects go missing for days on end before suddenly reappearing, and others just as inexplicably appear from nowhere and then vanish again. Coins, glasses, books and crockery seem to be favourites for poltergeists to treat in this way. A few poltergeists progress to more dangerous and frightening antics such as setting fire to furniture, scribbling obscene graffiti on walls or smashing household objects and windows. Generally a poltergeist attack lasts only a few weeks or a handful of months, a visitation enduring for more than a year, as did that at the York Arms, is rather unusual.

Exactly what causes a poltergeist outbreak is unclear. Sceptics have argued that the manifestations are invented or faked by the family that is afflicted, but some victims are genuinely distressed so this would seem not to be the solution. Traditionally, Yorkshire folk have explained poltergeist activity as taking place when a mischievous fairy or bogle takes up temporary residence in a house.

More recently, investigators into the paranormal have noticed some strong similarities between the majority of poltergeist cases. For a start it seems that the activity is focussed not on a house or property, but on a person. When that person is absent the activity ceases, and may follow the person if they go to stay elsewhere for a few days. Typically this focus person is a teenager, usually a girl, who is undergoing emotional stress of some kind, perhaps an unhappy romance or difficult exams. Not all poltergeists conform to this pattern, at least one centred on a man in his forties, but most do.

Some think the poltergeist activity is caused by a malignant or mischievous spirit that is attracted to the focus person and somehow uses them to break through into the mortal world. The word 'poltergeist' is German for 'noisy ghost' and was coined largely as a result of this theory. Others think that the focus person is him or herself unwittingly causing the trouble. The emotional problems are directed outward from the person by some form of telekinetic power that allows the person to move objects by thought power alone, albeit unconsciously. In fact nobody really knows what causes these mysterious, disturbing and at times downright terrifying outbreaks.

Aura of the Ghostly Child at Precentor's Court

After visiting the York Arms, you should continue north-west up what is now High Petergate to find the mighty gateway of Bootham Bar. If you turn right into a snickleway immediately before the gate you will find yourself entering Precentor's Court. One of the houses in this little court has long been rumoured to be haunted. The ghost manifests itself only when the house is empty. If a person should knock on the door at such a time, the door may be opened by the ghost of a young girl, aged around eight. This phantom child manages to emit an aura or atmosphere that is so powerful, and so deeply frightening, that those who encounter it almost invariably flee at once. When they summon up the courage to return, the door is locked and no amount of hammering will cause the child to reappear – until next time.

Precentor's Court has a little ghost, which at first sight may appear to be rather charming, but she soon reveals herself to be among the most terrifying in the city.

The Phantom Nun of Bootham Bar

Retrace your steps to Bootham Bar where a phantom nun has been seen. Just inside the gate itself the street has, along one side, a row of old buildings, now shops. These days the upper storeys are used as offices, either for the shops beneath or rented out to other businesses. As a result nobody is in them late at night, so nobody is there to encounter the ghost. In past years, the upper floors served as the homes of the families who owned and ran the shops at ground level, so the phantom was reported rather more often.

Inside one of the shops there was a ghost that was never seen, but which often made its presence felt. It would enter the front door, causing the bell attached to the door to ring, then walk across the ground floor. The ghostly intruder would then open the door at the rear of the shop and begin climbing the stairs. At the landing on the first floor, the footsteps would pause as if the spectre were trying to decide what to do next. Then they would be heard again, climbing up the next flight of stairs toward the second floor. After arriving on the second floor landing the footsteps would stop again, but this time not restart.

The ghostly footsteps were heard time and time again during the 1920s and 1930s. It was always assumed that it was the ghost of a woman who was making the sounds, as the footsteps seemed to be those of somebody in high heels on the wooden floor of the shop, and on the

The ancient gatehouse of Bootham Bar is a medieval structure, but it stands on the site of the original Roman gate that gave access to the fortress built here in AD 79. The area around the gate is said to be haunted by a nun.

The row of shops where an invisible spectre has been heard entering and leaving.

stairs sounded lighter than those made by most men. However, no story has ever been attached to the property that might explain the haunting. And since the ghost has only ever been heard, not seen, her identity must remain a mystery.

A Soft, Yellow Glow on the Staircase at Bootham

Just outside the gateway you will enter Bootham, the long road heading north out of York. This section of the road follows the exact route of the main Roman road that ran from York to Hadrian's Wall and the untamed barbarian lands beyond. Just outside the gateway is an old house that has been converted into two shops. At the back of one shop, out of sight of customers, is the grand staircase that served the house when it was a home. This staircase is haunted by the footsteps of some invisible intruder. This haunting has the added refinement that the ghost seems to carry a candle. When the footsteps pass by at night the soft, yellow glow of a candle is also seen.

These two shops in Bootham used to be one house, and the grand staircase from its days as a home is haunted by an invisible presence, which clumps upstairs with regularity.

All in Black: Attending Their Own Funeral at St Olave's Church

Continue on along Bootham until you reach Marygate on the left, marked by a massive round tower. Head down Marygate to find St Olave's Church. This is a charming little place of worship that goes back centuries. The ghosts, however, date back only to the Edwardian period of the early twentieth century. They take the form of a woman dressed in black mourning clothes as if attending a funeral, and a boy aged about 11 or so who is smartly dressed in dark grey jacket and tie. The two are usually seen sitting in a pew near the back of the church. They sit quietly and hardly move, as if attending a church service. The boy is visibly upset, seeming to cry, while the woman seeks to comfort him. When they have been in sight for a few seconds they fade from view. Nobody knows who they are nor for what reason they are so upset, though it is reasonable to assume from their clothes that they might be attending a funeral – perhaps their own.

St Olave's Church is home to a pair of ghosts, which date back about a century.

The Grey Lady of St Peter's School

Return to Bootham. If you feel energetic you should turn left and set off for St Peter's School, about half a mile distant. The pavement outside the school is said to be haunted by a grey lady. Grey ladies are insubstantial wraiths, which are reported from many different places. In some locations they have been identified by researchers to occur only on chilly evenings or dawns when mist might be expected to rise from nearby streams or springs. There are no nearby streams here so the grey lady must be presumed to be a genuine phantom, though who she might be remains obscure.

There is another spectre inside the school. This ghost is seen only in the loft of the school chapel. It is the phantom of a teenage boy dressed in pyjamas and red slippers. He is traditionally said to be the ghost of a pupil who was up in the loft early one morning for some unknown reason of his own. He leaned over the rail to peer down into the chapel, missed his footing and fell to his death. Such is the story, but the school history has no record of such a fatal accident. Like the ghostly lady outside, his identity must remain a mystery.

A Royal Lady and a Noble Wraith at King's Manor

If you don't feel like the expedition to the school, turn right and return toward the gateway at the end of Bootham. Just before the gateway, turn right to find yourself facing across an open square with the art gallery on the right and the iron railings around King's Manor straight in front.

This is probably the most haunted building in all of York. King's Manor dates back to 1208 when St Mary's Abbey was flush with funds from its rolling estates. The abbot decided that he needed a new house in which to entertain guests, and so began building this fine half-timbered structure resting on stone lower walls. In those days abbeys, such as St Mary's, were major landowners and played a significant role in both the economy and politics of the time. When war came, these religious houses even sent men to fight the king's wars. Wealthy merchants and noblemen came to do business with the abbeys, while kings and courtiers would often choose to visit them. Clerics and clergy were expected to play a full role in the administration of the kingdom, running local courts and supervising the collection of taxes. It was to provide a venue for such activity, rather than to give themselves lavish homes, that many abbots built large houses with bedrooms for guests and rooms where meetings could be held and paperwork completed.

It should come as no surprise, therefore, that one of the ghosts encountered in this monastic building is that of a lady. This ghostly lady wears a green dress and carries a bunch of roses in her hands. The dress seems to put the lady very firmly in the early or mid-sixteenth century. She walks with a stately tread, and the sounds of swishing and rustling, as if heavy silk is being moved, is often heard.

No doubt this phantom lady was a visitor to the house, though her fashion does not make it entirely certain if she would have come here before or after the Reformation saw the structure removed from ownership of St Mary's Abbey. While there is no firm evidence as to who this slim, dark-haired young lady might be, local tradition has it that she is none other than Anne Boleyn, the ill-fated second wife of Henry VIII.

King's Manor is probably the most actively haunted house in York. Much of the house is open to the public though it is owned by the university and is used by students.

It is known that Anne stayed at King's Manor for a short period when she was queen, and Henry was on one of his periodic journeys around the kingdom. These progressions allowed the king to inspect first hand the administration of his kingdom, looking over the financial books of his underlings in the counties, ensuring justice was being dispensed fairly to all and making sure that nobody was becoming so disaffected as to consider rebellion. The journeys also had the benefit of allowing the king to stay with his more affluent subjects at their expense, and so save the royal household expenditure on food and drink for a while. As a major landowner, the abbot of St Mary's, York, would have been expected to play host to the king and queen when they came to their great northern city.

So far as is known, Anne had no earlier link to the house, but this is not certain. Before she became queen she was the younger daughter of a fairly junior nobleman and few people would have paid much attention to her movements. It is known that she was given a liberal education and that she travelled widely, living in France for at least a year at one point. She also had a romance with Henry Percy, heir to the Earl of Northumberland. Whether this romance progressed so far as an engagement is unknown, but it was almost certainly chaste. It is possible that she came north at some stage to spend time with the Percy family and, if so, more than likely that she would have stopped at St Mary's Abbey when passing through York.

Whoever the lady in green might be, no such doubt exists about the ghost who haunts the staircase in the north wing. This is the wraith of Sir Henry Hastings. Sir Henry was a scion of the family that has held the title Earl of Huntingdon since George Hastings was granted the title by Henry VIII in 1529. It was Sir Henry who had the staircase constructed, and it is generally presumed that it is his ghost that haunts it. Certainly the ghost, with its buckled shoes, riding breeches and long jacket, wears fashions from the right era.

Interestingly there is a portrait of an unidentified gentleman in Stuart dress hanging in a room near the head of the staircase. During the 1930s and 1940s, this portrait was often found lying on the floor. It had quite clearly not fallen from the wall as it was always undamaged. It was as if unseen hands had lifted it off its hook and lain it gently on the floor. Speculation was rife that the portrait was of Sir Henry and that it was his ghost that was moving it. The portrait does not seem to have moved of its own accord for some years now, though the ghost remains as active as ever.

The ghostly woman who walks about King's Manor is usually said to be Anne Boleyn,
shown here in a Victorian engraving based on a contemporary portrait by Holbein.

A group of Roundhead soldiers. The ghosts of the wounded Parliamentarians from the Battle of Marston Moor haunt the courtyard of King's Manor, where they were brought for medical treatment.

The courtyard at the manor is haunted by ghosts that date to a time between that of Anne Boleyn and Sir Henry Hastings. In 1644 York was a staunchly Royalist city at a time when the fortunes of Parliament were on the rise in the English Civil War. When the Scottish government declared itself to be siding with the English Parliament, a Scottish army marched south over the border to lay siege to York. There was already one army of the English Parliament active in Yorkshire under Sir Thomas Fairfax, and this marched to support the Scottish siege. Oliver Cromwell, with his East Anglian army, rightly guessed that King Charles would seek to lift the siege of his wealthy northern city and so marched north to reinforce the besiegers.

On 1 July the Royalist army arrived to lift the siege, led by Prince Rupert. Rupert had with him only 25,000 men to face the 35,000 Parliamentarians, but he began with a brilliant tactical march that brought him round to the rear of the enemy army on Marston Moor. The battle that followed was long, drawn out and bloody, but the Royalists had lost it the moment that the Earl of Newcastle disobeyed Rupert and led his men in the wrong direction. Rupert extracted the defeated Royalist army with skill, rallying it at Richmond before marching south to report the failure to his king.

Fairfax marched on York and demanded its immediate surrender. Governor Sir Thomas Glemham refused and slammed the gates. He kept Fairfax outside for two weeks, until Fairfax was forced to agree to lenient terms of surrender. It was for this reason that the hundreds of Parliamentarian wounded were unable to seek shelter in the city. Instead large numbers were brought to King's Manor. There was not enough room for them all inside, so dozens were laid out on beds of straw to rest in the courtyard. Many died of infected wounds, and it is these unfortunates who haunt the courtyard still.

The final ghost at King's Manor is the oldest of them all. The figure of a man in black with a cowl covering his head has been seen many times in the oldest part of the building. This is undoubtedly a monk who dates back to the days when the house formed part of St Mary's Abbey. His name is unknown, but then a man who had devoted his entire life to the service of God might prefer it that way.

Ghostly Hauntings of the Black Abbot at St Mary's Abbey

In the grounds of the museum lie the ruins of St Mary's Abbey church. In medieval times the manor and church both stood within the walled enclosure of the abbey which projected west from the city walls themselves just south of Bootham Bar and along the north bank of the Ouse. Although ruined, the abbey church is still impressive and its shattered stones give a good idea of what an impressive building this must have been in its medieval heyday.

Some at least of its former residents have not left. There are persistent reports of a ghostly monk being seen among the ruins. Locally, the phantom is referred to as the Black Abbot, though since all the monks at the abbey would have worn black robes his identification as an abbot is uncertain.

The Ghost in the Tight Trousers at the Yorkshire Museum

Running up the left side of King's Manor is a narrow drive that leads alongside the beautiful house and passes through a gateway into the grounds of the Yorkshire Museum which is itself haunted, albeit by a ghost considerably younger than the Black Abbot. The sightings of this ghost began in 1954 when the caretaker glimpsed a figure in the library section of the museum. Knowing that nobody was supposed to be there except himself, the caretaker went to investigate, but he found the room to be empty of any human. At first the caretaker did not mention the sighting in case of ridicule, but over the following few years others saw the phantom.

The ghost was consistently described as being that of an elderly man dressed in fairly tight trousers and a knee-length coat or long jacket. Some said that he sported a top hat, but not everyone reported this headgear. When news of the haunting leaked out, a group of local men got permission to stay in the library overnight. At first they neither saw nor experienced anything at all unusual. They persisted, however, and one Sunday evening were rewarded by hearing a loud thud come from the empty library. Hurrying into the room they saw that a book had fallen from a shelf. They noted the time to be 8.40 p.m. They had no way of knowing if the book had fallen from the shelf because it had been put there insecurely or if it had been pushed by ghostly hands. They recorded that the book was a seemingly unimportant Victorian tome entitled *The Antiquities and Curiosities of the Church*. The book was replaced.

A few weeks later the caretaker heard a thud at 8.40 p.m. He too found that a book had fallen from a shelf. It was *The Antiquities and Curiosities of the Church*. When the same book fell

The Yorkshire Museum is home to a ghost with a fascination with one particular book kept in the library.

at the same time on a third evening, the interested gentlemen decided to investigate. The book was recorded as having been presented to the museum by an Alderman Edward Wooler from Darlington. The Wooler family was contacted and a photograph of the deceased alderman was acquired. When this was shown to the caretaker he unhesitatingly identified the dead worthy as being the ghost of the library.

The book was then studied for any clue as to why the phantom alderman attached such importance to it. None of the 'antiquities and curiosities' mentioned in the book seemed to have any link to the Wooler family and no sections had been underlined or marked in any way. There was, however, a faint rectangular outline on the inside front cover as if a photograph or document had been habitually lodged there. Whatever had made the mark was no longer there, but perhaps it was this which attracted the ghostly man. We shall never know.

Walled up Alive: The Grey Lady of The Theatre Royal

Leaving the abbey ruins and the Yorkshire Museum, return back along the drive to King's Manor. Then turn right into St Leonard's Place, going past the museum and St Mary's Abbey to reach the Theatre Royal. This fine structure is the haunt of one of the best known and best attested ghosts in the city, the Grey Lady.

The ruins of St Mary's Abbey are, perhaps predictably, haunted by a ghostly monk.

This particular grey lady is usually identified as being a medieval nun who fell in love with a citizen of York. According to the best known version of this tale, the nun fell pregnant and tried to get away from the hospital to be with her lover. However, she was apprehended and, when the reason for her attempted flight was discovered, the spiritual authorities decided to make an example of her. Ecclesiastical authorities were not allowed to spill blood, but they could inflict death by other means. The unfortunate nun was walled up alive and left to die a terrible, lingering death.

The site was, before the Reformation, occupied by a part of St Leonard's Hospital, where nuns cared for the sick and injured of the city who could not afford medical treatment for themselves. Certainly nuns did live here, though the records of the hospital were lost at the Reformation so there is no way of knowing if the traditional tale has any basis in fact. Several buildings have come and gone since then, the present theatre being erected in late Victorian times. If the identification of the phantom is correct, it would seem that the ghost of the nun has endured through all these changes. On the other hand, the Grey Lady may date from a more recent period. Her outfit of long grey dress and pale headscarf or coif would not be out of place in many different periods.

She has been seen in most parts of the theatre over the years, though she seems to prefer the downstairs areas as a rule. One time when she broke that habit came in 1974 when the theatre was about to put on a production of the play *Dear Octopus*. The cast were on stage going through a final rehearsal when one of the actors missed his lines. The others waited,

The Theatre Royal is home to one of the best known phantoms in York: the Grey Lady.

but he made no attempt to continue, indeed he was not paying them the slightest bit of attention but was gazing intently out into the auditorium. Following his gaze, the others saw a glowing light hovering in the middle of the Dress Circle. The light looked as if it were a low-powered bulb shining through a thick cloth, like a lantern in a tent. Slowly the vague glow began to assume definite shape and form. It was the Grey Lady sitting in a seat, looking down on the stage. The astonished cast did not have time to react before the phantom abruptly vanished. The ghost has since been seen up in the Dress Circle again, but she still prefers downstairs.

There are some who believe that the Grey Lady may have left the Theatre Royal for good. In the mid-1980s a séance was held in the theatre in the hope of contacting the spirit of the phantom nun. The medium claimed that she was able to talk to the nun, but the tale that emerged was rather different from the traditional one. The medium said that the spirit claimed that in life she had been a fun-loving and vivacious young woman, but not that she had committed any sins of the flesh. Instead she had played japes and jokes on her fellow sisters, and these had gone down badly. After one service the nun claimed to have seen angels hovering over the altar, and was locked up in her room as a punishment for having a black and lying tongue – none of the other nuns having seen the celestial host. It was not entirely clear from the account either how the nun had died or why she haunted the theatre built on the site of her old home.

There then followed a short ceremony designed to bring peace to the soul of the nun and allow her to pass on in peace. Whether or not that worked is unclear.

The Grey Lady is not the only phantom in the Theatre Royal. A theatre was first built here in 1740, and it is to this earlier structure that this ghost belongs. Sometime in the 1770s or 1780s the leading actor of the show took a fancy to one of the chorus girls. The actor was tall, dark and good looking with a penchant for fine clothes and he sported a large emerald ring. He was known for his wayward eye, though his conquests never had any cause to complain that he did not spend lavishly on them while the affair lasted.

Whether or not this particular young lady welcomed his advances, she was already spoken for. The existing beau naturally resented the actor's attentions and this led to a quarrel. That quarrel took place one afternoon in nearby Blake Street; it turned violent and ended with the actor being stabbed in the chest. The actor died and his killer was arrested for murder.

That, of course, left the theatre management with the problem of what to do about that evening's show. True to the tradition of the stage that 'the show must go on', it was decided to

One of several roundels on the façade of the Theatre Royal.

go ahead with the show with the understudy taking the role of the leading man. All went well until just moments before the curtain was due to go up, when the ghost of the murdered man strode on to the stage to take up his opening position. The aghast company were on the verge of panic when the apparition vanished. The manager came down to steady their nerves and the show did indeed go on, albeit understandably late.

The ghostly actor with the emerald ring was a familiar spectral figure throughout the nineteenth and early twentieth centuries and was seen dozens of times. He then was not seen for some decades until he put in a single appearance in the 1960s. He has not been seen since.

The final ghostly manifestation at the Theatre Royal is rather more enigmatic. Several people have reported hearing the faint strains of organ music in the building. There is not, and never has been, an organ in the building.

The Shadow of the Drowned: Lendal Bridge

Leaving the theatre, continue along St Leonard's Place to its end. Then turn right into Museum Street and cross the River Ouse via Lendal Bridge to enter Station Road. While crossing the river, glance to your right. It is along the northern bank in this area that the shadowy figure of a woman dressed in black has been seen. She is generally thought to be the spectre of a woman who drowned in the river many years ago, but who or when is unknown. This is the type of explanation that sometimes springs up to explain an apparition about which nothing is, in fact, known. Perhaps the unfortunate lady in black did drown, but it may be that she is simply some wayward ghost whose proximity to the river led to the story.

The Ouse seen from Lendal Bridge. The north bank is haunted by the enigmatic figure of a lady in black.

'Impossible to Put into Words': The National Railway Museum

On the far side of the bridge you could, if you are feeling energetic, take an excursion to the National Railway Museum, which lies about two thirds of a mile away. Turn right into Station Avenue. Do not bear right into the station itself, but continue straight on into Leeman Road, cross the railway bridge and find the museum on your right. There is, of course, a charge for entry, but for those interested in railway history it is a price well worth paying to enter this magnificent collection of trains, carriages and railway paraphernalia of all kinds.

The interest for those looking for ghosts lies in one of the old sleeping cars preserved here. A strange figure has been seen in the carriage, peering out at the museum-goers who pass by. He is described as being smartly dressed in suit and tie of an old-fashioned cut, but those who have seen him insist that there is 'something odd' about him. Quite what is apparently impossible to put into words, but it certainly rather disquieting.

If you do not fancy the excursion to the Railway Museum do not turn right into Station Avenue, but turn left into Rougier Street, then take the first right into Tanner Row, which becomes Toft Green and bears left to become Bar Lane. At the end of Bar Lane turn sharp right to find the towering stone mass of Micklegate Bar.

Lost Keys and Spiked Heads at Micklegate Bar

This imposing gateway was, in former times, the place where the heads of traitors were set up on spikes to deter others from following in their footsteps. The heads were put on long wooden poles that were set upright into sockets on either side of the central stone figure on the battlements. Over the years many dozens of unfortunate men have been executed and had their heads spiked here, but as far as is known only two deaths have led to a haunting. The first was the execution of Thomas Percy, Earl of Northumberland, in 1572, though we shall be meeting his phantom elsewhere in the city.

The second was the execution of twenty-two Jacobite rebels who had taken up arms to support Bonny Prince Charlie in 1745. Of these, only two were selected to have their heads spiked. In 1754 the heads vanished one night. It was later found that a Catholic tailor named William Arundell had stolen them and given them burial out of compassion for his fellow Catholics. The government feared that Arundell's actions might encourage other Catholics to show sympathy for the Jacobite cause and came down hard on the tailor. He was sent to prison for two years, fined £5 and ordered to hand over a surety of £200 against his future good conduct. For some reason the feelings of inexplicable terror and horror that overwhelm some visitors to Micklegate Bar are often put down to the hapless Jacobites whose heads were spiked here.

Another ghost of Micklegate Bar is a monk who has been seen on the city walls close to the gate.

By far the best known and most active of the ghosts that may be encountered here is that of a young lady named Sarah Brocklebank. Back in 1797 it was still the custom for the gates to the city to be locked each evening as the curfew bell tolled and for them to be reopened again at dawn the next day. The days when raiding armies of Scots might seek to launch a surprise

The towering mass of Micklegate Bar is home to one of the most tragic phantoms to lurk in the city.

nocturnal attack were by then long gone, and increasingly effective forces of law and order were making gangs of armed robbers less dangerous, although the practice was still continuing.

The locking of Micklegate Bar was the duty of one Thomas Brocklebank, who lived in the tower with his family and was paid a small wage for performing his nightly task. His daughter was the lively teenage Sarah, who often stood in for her father and worked in the city. On her birthday in 1797, Sarah invited some friends to the towered gateway. The young people spent the day playing all sorts of games and generally larking about. When sunset drew on, Thomas went to lock the gates, but the keys were nowhere to be found.

The father suspected either his daughter or one of her friends of playing a foolish prank. He turned on his daughter, and set her the task of finding the keys. The gates were shut and propped closed with a wooden beam. Sarah could not find the key anywhere. The next day her friends were summoned and each solemnly denied having moved, hidden or stolen the keys to Micklegate Bar. Eventually Thomas had to confess to the city authorities that the keys were missing. He was sacked from his job on the spot and thrown out of his imposing home. He never spoke to his daughter again.

Thereafter, Sarah spent every spare moment she had searching for the lost keys to Micklegate Bar. As the years passed she became a well known and rather pathetic figure in the city. When not at work she would spend her days poking about in rubbish tips, prying into nooks and crannies and always seeking those lost keys.

Forty years later the then Mayor of York was entertaining some local worthies in his parlour when the sounds of a commotion outside reached them. The door was thrown open and in came the now aging Sarah Brocklebank. She stared at the mayor and declared in a loud clear voice, 'Have found them.' The years seemed to fall away from the frail, middle-aged lady as if her lost youth were returning to her. 'Have found them,' she said again. And then she dropped down dead. Wherever she had found the keys, they remain there still.

A waxwork of the unfortunate Sarah can be seen to this day in one of the upstairs rooms of Micklegate Bar, now a museum. The waxwork grips in her left hand a set of large, ancient keys. Sarah is identified as the female ghost in a long dress who is seen here from time to time. She is also blamed for the frequent reports made by visitors of an invisible and deathly cold hand that is laid on their shoulders as they look around the Bar.

Eternal Love and a Broken Heart at the Punch Bowl Pub

Just outside the Bar is the Punch Bowl pub. The cellar is, apparently, haunted by a large man in an apron. He is said to be a former landlord who died on the premises and presumably loved the place so much that he cannot bear to leave. There is also a rather less solid phantom of a woman who is seen upstairs. She is sometimes said to have been a young woman who lived here in centuries gone by and who died of a broken heart after some tragic romance. Whether she is linked to the landlord in the cellar is unclear.

The Punch Bowl pub just beside Micklegate Bar is haunted by a man thought to be a former landlord of this excellent inn.

A Column of Ice-Cold Mist Which Sucks all the Warmth from the Air: The Phantom Ostler of the Windmill Hotel

Continue to walk south-west along Blossom Street to find the Windmill Hotel on the right at No. 14. The ghost here is usually said to be that of an eighteenth-century ostler. He is not seen very often, but when he does appear he most certainly does seem to be wearing clothes that would fit with such a date and occupation. He has, on occasion, been mistaken for a workman. Perhaps the best documented case of this came when a cleaner was going up the stairs and spotted, as she thought, a builder coming down. The pub at this time was having some building work done, so her assumption was a natural one. The cleaner stepped aside to let the burly figure pass her. At that moment she thought that there was something odd about the man, and simultaneously wondered what a builder supposed to be working in the yard would be doing upstairs. She turned to accost the man, but he had gone. She hurried downstairs, but the place was empty.

The phantom of the Windmill is heard more often than he is seen, but when he does appear he seems to be a remarkably solid apparition.

The ghostly ostler has also been blamed for the heavy, phantom footsteps that are heard climbing the staircase. Interestingly, the ghostly sounds are unmistakably those of a man's boots thudding up wooden stairs even though the staircase is carpeted and has been for many years. This same ghost is also held to be responsible for the ice-cold mist that sometimes forms on the upper corridor. This strange mist takes the form of a column about six feet tall and some three feet across. Those who have encountered it say that it seems to suck all the warmth out of the air, leaving the room as cold as a deep freeze, even on the warmest summer days.

Finally, it is worth mentioning that in the 1970s, the then landlord hired a new barman who proved to be efficient, hard-working and popular with customers. Sadly the man had been in post only a week or so when he one day marched up to the landlord and announced that he was leaving. 'I'm not staying here, not with what else is here,' the man said and left never to return.

Another, rather older, story about the Windmill maintains that there is a second ghost to be met just outside the front door. This sad little phantom is said to be the ghost of a little girl who was knocked down and killed by a horse and cart in the mid-nineteenth century. This particular phantom has not been seen for a good many years. Perhaps, as is the way with many ghosts, she has faded from human view.

Reuniting the Spirits: Church of the Holy Trinity

Leaving the Windmill, return back through Micklegate Bar and continue straight on along Micklegate to the Church of the Holy Trinity on the right. There is no doubt about the fact that this church is haunted, or about what form the ghosts take. The explanation for them is, however, shrouded in mystery as there are two entirely different stories to account for them. The ghosts are most certainly of two women and a young girl. The girl is usually seen in the company of one of the women, while the other woman is usually seen alone. The lone phantom is reported to be that of an old woman, while the two seen together are of an age to be mother and daughter. These two are said to wear clothing that would date them to the seventeenth century, though the older woman wears a plain, long dress that might belong to almost any era.

The first story about these phantoms has it that the mother and child are from a family that worshipped here. The child, it would seem, was one of the many unfortunates at that date who died young and so was buried here. The mother, however, then died and was buried many miles away. The older woman, according to this tale, is the grandmother of the family. She has intervened in death to reunite the mother and daughter whose earthly bodies are separated by so great a distance, but whose spirits can now be together.

The quite different version has it that the older woman is the last abbess of the medieval convent that had ownership of this church before the Reformation. When Henry VIII's men came to wrest possession of the church from the convent they found the abbess busily engaged in trying to empty the church of its plate, manuscripts and other treasures so that they could be kept from the greedy grasp of the monarch. The royal commissioners ran to intervene and a scuffle broke out in which the abbess was killed.

It is a good story, but it must be admitted that so far as is known no nuns, still less an abbess, were murdered during the dissolution of the monasteries and convents that took place during

The gates that give access to the churchyard of Holy Trinity, Micklegate.

Henry VIII's reign in the early sixteenth century. Most of those living in holy orders were given a pension for life and left their establishments peacefully, if not always happily. A few were actually enthusiastic advocates of the suppression of the monasteries as they had converted to the new Protestant faith. There were, it is true, some who objected to the changes and there were several outbreaks of violence involving monks, a handful of whom died. Nuns, it seems, did not fight back, which was probably wise given the size and arms of the men sent to take possession of the nunneries. Of course, just because no record survives of a murdered nun, it does not mean that no nun died. Perhaps there was a fatality here, or maybe a nun died soon after being turned out, and in popular imagination her death was blamed on the royal commissioners.

According to this story, the mother and daughter have absolutely no connection at all to the older abbess. Instead they are said to date back to one of the outbreaks of plague that affected York in the seventeenth century. Whether the daughter died of the plague and the mother then succumbed to a broken heart, or if the mother perished first depends on which version you listen to. Either way, it was a tragic double blow to some York family.

Holy Trinity, Micklegate, is haunted by three ghosts who are thought to be linked, but it is not entirely clear how they are connected.

Ghosts on the BBC: The Ghost Dancer of Bishophill

At the far end of the Holy Trinity churchyard, turn right into Trinity Street. Go straight over the crossroads, then take the next right into Bishophill. On the right is a former church hall, which was sold by the Church of England some years ago and has since been used as a storeroom, dance school and shop. It is to its days as a dance school that the haunting dates.

The ghostly lady who haunts this place is generally identified as having been one of the dance teachers who taught here in the 1950s and 1960s. The lady has been seen several times in the corridor that leads from the front door through to the main hall. She often appears to be in a great hurry, bustling along with swift steps. One witness said that she thought the ghost was hostile, or at least angry, but most take her to be rather gentle.

Whatever her mood or intentions, the ghost has been blamed for a wide assortment of unusual happenings in the building. The back doors that lead from the hall to a small garden will sometimes shudder and rattle as if they are being vigorously shaken by unseen hands. Furniture is sometimes found in the morning to have been moved around during the night. Books fall from shelves and pools of water appear from nowhere. So famous did the ghostly happenings become that the BBC sent a news crew to interview staff and film the premises. Nothing supernatural was caught on camera, but the television crew did not entirely escape the attentions of the

The former church hall in Bishophill, which hit the headlines in the 1960s because of its spectacular haunting.

phantom. Their recording equipment and cameras persistently malfunctioned and refused to operate property. They had been fine before the crew arrived, and worked perfectly after they had left. It was only while they were in the hall that the equipment would not work.

'Who Never Said a Foolish Thing – Nor Never Did a Wise One': A Malevolent Presence at the Cock and Bottle

Return back along Bishophill, and Trinity Street to return to Micklegate. Turn right at Micklegate and continue downhill as Micklegate becomes Bridge Street. A few yards before the road reaches the River Ouse, turn right into Skeldergate. In this street stands what is without doubt the most famous haunted pub in York: the Cock and Bottle.

This delightful and welcoming pub already had a reputation for being haunted before the Second World War, but nobody kept any detailed accounts of the supernatural activity until Peter and Brenda Stanley took over as managers in 1973. Until that time there were assorted tales of a ghostly man in old-fashioned clothes, spectral footsteps and the sound of a wooden door being broken down. The Stanleys were very quickly made aware of their ghostly residents when a picture fell off the wall several times the day after they moved in. Having been told by locals of the supposed ghost, the Stanleys decided to keep a diary of events.

For the most part, the Stanleys' supernatural diary recorded events as being much the same as they had earlier been alleged. The sound of a wooden door being smashed open came several times, and with great volume. The phantom footsteps also manifested themselves several times, usually in the same downstairs bar room as the noises of the smashing door. They also recorded the more insubstantial, but considerably more unnerving, sense of great and impending evil. This feeling will come over a person quite suddenly, and one man was rooted to the spot in terror for a few seconds. It is as if something deeply malevolent has suddenly entered the room with the intention of wrecking havoc. Fortunately the feeling rarely lasts longer than a few seconds and goes as quickly as it comes.

Perhaps most interesting was the fact that Mrs Stanley not only saw the spectral man on more than one occasion, but got a very good look at him. She was able to give a clear description of the ghost. He was, she said, of average height with dark, wavy hair falling to his shoulders. He had a big nose and was, she thought, fairly ugly. He was dressed in a long jacket with lots of buttons and embroidered buttonholes. At once the hunt was on for a former owner or resident who would match this description. It was not long before the local press had found that the site of the Cock and Bottle had formerly been occupied by a workshop owned by George Villiers, Duke of Buckingham, in the later seventeenth century. A portrait of the gentleman was acquired and, while Mrs Stanley could not be certain, it did seem to match her description.

The most famous haunted pub in York is undoubtedly the Cock and Bottle in Skeldergate.

If the ghost is that of Buckingham, then it is the ghost of a quite remarkable man who led an astonishing life. Villiers was born in 1628, son of George Villiers, 1st Duke of Buckingham. When young George was only seven months old, his father was assassinated by a religious fanatic and he inherited the vast wealth that went with the title. He also inherited his father's intelligence, wit and devastating charm. As the orphaned son of a duke, young George was taken under the wing of King Charles I. He grew up with the king's children and so became a lifelong friend of the prince who would become King Charles II. As teenagers the two young men embarked on a variety of escapades that usually involved drink and loose women, much to the annoyance of Charles' father.

When the English Civil War broke out, Charles was too young and too valuable to be allowed to risk his life in battle. George was a few years older, however, and was thought mature enough to fight. He fought bravely and well, but achieved no great victories. When the Royalists were defeated and Charles I executed, Buckingham went into exile with Prince Charles. For this act, Parliament stripped the young Duke of Buckingham of all his estates and property, thus reducing him to penury. Buckingham rode with Charles on the campaign that ended in disaster at the Battle of Worcester in 1651, and fled into exile once again.

For the time being it looked as if Prince Charles might live out his entire life as an exiled king without a kingdom. Buckingham retained Charles's friendship, but decided that he had to try to make his way in the world. After failing get employment at various courts around Europe, Buckingham returned to England under an assumed name. Posing as a European gentleman, he mingled with the new men who ruled Britain under Parliament. Among his acquaintances was the daughter of Sir Thomas Fairfax, the victor of the Battle of Marston Moor and one of the most respected generals in Europe. Fairfax had fallen out with Oliver Cromwell and Parliament when he objected to the execution of Charles I and, by the time Buckingham arrived on the scene, had retired to his estates in Yorkshire.

The young woman fell deeply in love with Buckingham and, after he had revealed his true identity, Fairfax agreed to use his influence to have the young man pardoned. This he achieved, but the Buckingham estates were still denied him. When the young couple married, however, Buckingham stood to inherit a reasonable amount of Yorkshire land and money through his wife and might have been content. But in 1658 Cromwell died and two years later Parliament invited Prince Charles to return as King Charles II. Now it was Buckingham's turn to do a favour to his new father-in-law, being instrumental in reconciling Fairfax to Charles.

With his old friend on the throne, Buckingham hurried off to London where the two men soon resumed their disreputable adventures. Charles restored Buckingham to his vast wealth and made him a key member of the government. By 1667 Buckingham was having an affair with the Countess of Shrewsbury. When the Earl of Shrewsbury learned of the affair, he called Buckingham out to a duel. The errant countess attended the duel disguised as a page and watched as her lover killed her husband. The resulting scandal forced Buckingham out of government, but he returned the following year.

Throughout his period in government, Buckingham found time not only to indulge in love affairs, but also to write plays and poems. He was famed for his wit and ability to produce humorous comments and ripostes. On one famous occasion his sharp tongue was turned against him by his friend Charles. At a dinner, Charles made some particularly clever remark prompting Buckingham to quip, 'All hail King Charles who never said a foolish thing – nor never did a wise one.'

Charles laughed and replied, 'That is true and just. For my words are my own, but my acts are those of my ministers.' Buckingham at the time was one of those ministers.

It was an exciting and successful life for Buckingham. So it came as a great shock to Charles and others when, in 1673, Buckingham suddenly announced that he was retiring. He had had enough, he said, of the glittering court life and craved some peace and quiet. He closed up his London home and rode north to York.

That was how he came to live in Skeldergate, inhabiting a grand house that has since been demolished. The garden of the house included the land on which the Cock and Bottle now stands and there stood a workshop. Buckingham had always been interested in science, and now he indulged his fancy. Buckingham ordered a mass of the most obscure chemicals and equipment from the apothecaries of York, and sent off to London for what he could not get locally. Clouds of coloured smokes emerged from the workshop, noxious smells filled the air and there were the occasional bangs. The good citizens of York looked askance at the workshop and at Buckingham. Some said he was trying to turn lead into gold, others that he was searching for the elixir of eternal youth and a few muttered that he was dabbling in witchcraft. His great charm and considerable wealth, however, won over most critics and ensured that those he could not charm were ignored.

Buckingham died in 1687 at his country house, a modest farm at Kirby Moorside, and his body was taken south to be buried in Westminster. Whether it is his ghost that lurks at the Cock and Bottle it is impossible to know for certain. However, in some ways it is to be hoped that the phantom of this colourful character remains at York to bring some excitement to the lives of its citizens.

The Shrine and the Spectral Cowl at Skeldergate Graveyard

Leaving the Cock and Bottle, turn right and walk about forty yards before turning right up an alleyway that runs between housing to reach a small graveyard. If you look carefully you should be able to make out in the turf the outlines of the little shrine that used to stand here. Many people have reported a feeling of great calm washing over them if they stand inside the demolished chapel. There have also been reports of a spectral cowled figure.

The Dark Caped Spectre of the Yorkshire Hussar

Return to Skeldergate and then back to the junction with Bridge Street. Go straight across to enter North Street to find another haunted pub, this time it is the Yorkshire Hussar that is home to a spectre.

Although the building is ancient, there was no hint of supernatural activity here until the 1970s when a new landlord came in the form of Colin Copeland. Colin decided that the place needed a few alterations, and a great deal of redecoration, before it would be suitable to welcome in the thirsty folk of York. It seems that, as is so often the case, the building work sparked the haunting.

The graveyard off Skeldergate is the haunt of a strange figure in a cloak and hood.

The alleyway that runs off Skeldergate, close to the Cock and Bottle.

The Yorkshire Hussar pub had not the slightest trace of supernatural activity until the 1970s, when a new landlord began building works that unleashed a spectre.

The first person to see the ghost was painter Terry Wright, who, along with his fellow decorator, Gordon Phillips, and two others, was working late in the bar. Copeland had offered the men a bonus if the work was finished early, so they were cheerfully putting in the extra hours. Wright was bending down to paint the bottom of a door in the main bar when he saw a tall man gliding across the room toward him dressed all in black with what seemed to be a cape slung over his shoulders.

The apparition so shocked Wright that he stood up abruptly and stepped back, tripping over a bench and falling back with a terrific crash. Phillips looked up from his work and likewise saw the ominous figure advancing toward him. He let out a cry of alarm which brought the other two men running. They arrived just in time to see the dark figure turn aside and walk into an apparently solid wall through which it vanished.

Unsurprisingly, all four men promptly fled the pub, though Phillips did have the presence of mind to lock the door behind them. The next day they told Copeland firmly that they would do no more work after dark. This meant that they forfeited their bonuses, but they preferred this to another encounter with the phantom.

In the course of their subsequent work, the men stripped the walls of the bar back to the bare plaster. They found that the spot where the ghost had vanished was the site of a

The very modern Park Inn Hotel is built on the site of an old haunted house, and some think the ghost may have survived the building work.

long-blocked-up doorway. Presumably the ghost was walking through the door that was there when it was alive, but which was gone by the time it was seen. The dark figure of the ghost has appeared off and on ever since.

A Returning Victim at the Park Inn Hotel

Just opposite from the Yorkshire Hussar pub stands the very modern Park Inn Hotel. One of the houses pulled down to make way for this imposing edifice was well known to be haunted. A murder had taken place there in Victorian times, and the ghost of the victim had walked in the house ever since. Most people hoped and expected that when the old house was bulldozed, the ghost would go with it. Not so, apparently. Since the hotel opened there have been persistent, but largely unconfirmed reports, that members of staff have seen a vague, shadowy figure of indistinct outline hovering about the place.

The soaring spire of the imposing Church of All Saints. The pavement outside is the haunt of a most gentle phantom.

A Gentle Ghost Pottering Along by the Church of All Saints

Further still along North Street on the left stands the beautiful and imposing Church of All Saints. The structure dates back to the 1340s and has a magnificent fifteenth-century roof. There is some medieval stained glass, and some twentieth-century additions that were carried out with sympathy and respect for the older parts of the building. The stretch of street between the church and Tanner Row is haunted by an elderly lady. This gentle soul does not harm anyone, but simply potters along to enter the railed garden there. Her clothes date her to about the time of the Second World War.

'A Gurgling, a Choking Cry and a Heavy Thud': Murder at Judge's Lodgings

The northern end of North Street bends left, becoming Wellington Row. Turn right at the junction with Museum Street and cross the River Ouse by way of Lendal Bridge.

The Judge's Lodging Hotel was, in the nineteenth century, the scene for a terrifyingly disturbed night for one visitor.

On the far bank turn sharp right into Lendal. Almost immediately you will come across the building known as Judge's Lodging. This is now a hotel, but was formerly used to provide accommodation for judges and other legal persons who were visiting York to take part in trials and other work.

During the nineteenth century the place became notorious among visiting lawyers for being haunted. One such visitor left a detailed account of his encounter with the supernatural. He had worked hard during the day and expected to sleep well. His room had a warm fire burning the grate, which cast a rosy glow over the room when he blew out his candle. He was soon asleep.

Some hours later he was suddenly awoken by something, but he did not know what. The fire had now died down and its ember barely illuminated the hearth, the rest of the room was in darkness. As he lay there, the man heard a nearby church clock strike two. He then heard the sound of footsteps moving stealthily across the room, and feared that an intruder had got in and was going to rifle through his pockets. The man was reaching out for his matches when he heard a voice from downstairs call out the name Henry. The footsteps abruptly halted.

Then came the sound of footsteps coming up the stairs. These gave the impression that the person making them was injured or crippled in some way, for one foot seemed to drag behind the other. The sounds came up the stairs, and entered the bedroom even though the door had not opened. The lawyer was by this point thoroughly terrified, but he listened as there came the sound of a scuffle and a short struggle, followed by a gurgling, choking cry and a heavy thud. Silence returned. The lawyer lit his match to find the room utterly empty.

Unsurprisingly he slept badly for the rest of the night. When dawn came he nodded off, only to be awakened by a maid knocking on the door and calling out that she had brought hot water. The lawyer scrambled out of bed to open the door, and was both astonished and terrified to find that it was bolted from the inside although he had left the bolt undone the night before.

The disturbances were generally put down to the suicide of a young man which had taken place some years earlier. However, local gossip had it that the man had not killed himself at all. It was said that he had been murdered by his uncle, a rich and influential judge. The truth is not known, and probably never will be, but the disturbances remain.

Time Slip at Davygate

Past the Judge's Lodging, turn left to pass through St Helen's Square to reach a junction with Blake Street on the left and Davygate on the right. Turn down Davygate, heading south-east.

In 1958 Davygate was the scene of what may have been a case of ghosts being seen only once, though other researchers think that the event was actually a time slip. Two women

The shopping street of Davygate was the scene of a frightening time slip or vision of the past, which involved a whole host of phantoms.

walking along the street from this junction toward Church Street suddenly saw the surrounding buildings shimmer and vanish to be replaced by open countryside in which a battle was taking place. As the alarmed women watched, Romans in armour surged past in formation to crash into a yelling mob of Celts, complete with war paint and ferociously spiked hair. The vision lasted seconds, then vanished.

What makes this vision interesting to historians is the location in which it took place. Excavations have shown that the walls of the original Roman fortifications stood just to the north of Davygate, so in the earliest days of the Roman occupation this stretch of land would have stood immediately outside the southern gate. If the fortress had ever come under attack, then the conventional tactics of the day would have made Davygate the scene of heavy fighting. Gates were the most vulnerable part of any Roman fortress and so would have attracted the

The ghostly Battle of Davygate was apparently between armoured Roman legionaries and more lightly equipped Celts, which would date the actual event to the first century AD.

attentions of an assaulting army. The Romans often waited until an attack had run its course, then launched a counterattack by opening the gates and storming forward in a dense formation to kill enemy wounded, break up their formation and chase them from the field. It seems that the women were describing just this sort of action.

The problem is that the detailed records for the history of the Roman legionary fortress at York were lost during the barbarian invasions that ended the Western Roman Empire. We simply do not know if any such battle ever raged around the southern gate of the fortress. There is, however, a well documented campaign of the Romans in Britain that almost certainly did involve a Celtic attack on the fortress at York.

Around AD 65, the Romans intended to occupy only the fertile areas of Britain south of the Humber and the Dee where they could produce large quantities of grain for export to the rest of the Empire. For defence they had three legions in Britain, plus auxiliaries, but relied mostly on having friendly tribes on the borders of the new province. Most of what is now Yorkshire, at least along the coast, was occupied by the Parisii tribe. What is now North Yorkshire, Durham, Northumberland and the Pennines was held by the much larger and more powerful Brigantes tribe. The Romans allied with Queen Cartimandua of the Brigantes, ensuring her loyalty with gifts and flattery.

For some unknown reason, however, a coup erupted among the Brigantes. Cartimandua was thrown out and a nobleman named Venutius took power. Venutius was determinedly anti-Roman. He began raiding into Roman territory and his agents spread across southern Britain, trying to foment revolt. The Roman governor, Petillius Cerialis, was given an extra legion and ordered to conquer the Brigantes. His first move was to send the IX Legion into the territory of the Parisii, both to secure their loyalty and to protect them from Brigante raids. The spot chosen by the IX for their fortress was the future site of York. In the spring of AD 71, the legion began work by building a ditch and wooden stockade around their tents, preparatory to more permanent defences and buildings.

We know that Venutius launched a pre-emptive strike on the IX Legion and that it failed. We don't know exactly where that battle was fought, but it seems likely that the Celts would have sought to drive the Romans back as soon as they realised that they were constructing a permanent fortress, and that would fight at York. Perhaps it was this battle that the two women glimpsed.

Phantom Bathers at the Roman Bath Pub

Continue down Davygate to reach a small open square on the left, Finkle Street. On the far side of the square you will see the Roman Bath public house. The pub is named after the extensive bathhouse that archaeologists found underneath this site during a dig. The finds are housed in a small museum in the pub's cellar that is well worth a visit.

Long before the historians found that this was the site of the military baths attached to the Roman fortress that stood just north of here, buildings on the site had been the home of some very odd noises. These were variously described as being the sound of splashing, water running over a fountain and burst pipes. No matter how much effort the property owners put into trying to find the supposed burst pipe or ruptured water main, nothing ever turned up. The sounds

The pub sign for the Roman Baths public house shows an imaginative recreation of the baths that once stood on this site.

continue still, but are now usually described as being the ghostly sounds of phantom bathers in the buried bath complex.

A Skull Under the Stairs at Stonegate

Leaving the pub, turn right to enter a narrow pedestrianised lane that runs north-west to end at a T-junction with Back Swinegate. Turn left into Back Swinegate, then follow it as it turns sharply to the right to become Little Stonegate and so continue in a north-westerly direction. This lane emerges at a second T-junction into Stonegate. You will be turning right along this street, but first you need to inspect some of the properties in the lane.

When building work was being carried out in one of the houses in this short street, a human skull was found tucked under the stairs. How long it had been there and to whom it had belonged was never discovered. However, those who lived there had long suspected that there

The shop that occupies No. 41 Stonegate has a sad little ghost who once startled staff by sitting on the serving counter.

was something odd about the staircase. Pets would not walk up it, and animals have long been rumoured to be more attuned to the supernatural than are humans.

The shop that occupies No. 41 is haunted by the sad little ghost of a six-year-old girl who died after falling down the stairs in the mid-Victorian period. She is seen, and heard, most often on the stairs but also puts in the occasional appearance in the shop itself. She was once seen sitting on the counter.

The other ghost of Stonegate actually belongs to the narrow Church Passage that opens off it. The man in the broad-brimmed black hat and black cloak whose phantom has been seen here is often identified as being Guy Fawkes, though why is not clear. Although he is best known for his role in the Gunpowder Plot of 1605, Fawkes had led a highly adventurous life before he was dragged to his death.

He was born in a house in High Petergate in 1570, the son of respectable Protestant parents from York's merchant community. His father died when he was nine and three years later his mother remarried, taking as husband Denis Bainbridge, a Catholic. It was probably his stepfather's influence that converted Fawkes to Catholicism and in his teenage years he became devoted to his new faith. After leaving school, Fawkes worked for a while as a servant to the Montagu family but when he inherited his father's wealth at the age of twenty-one he embarked on a new career. He sold up his inheritance for cash and used the money to equip himself as a soldier. Leaving England, Fawkes joined the Catholic Spanish army fighting against the Protestants in the Netherlands. He soon acquired a reputation as being an expert in the use of gunpowder for demolitions or blasting. By 1596 he was commanding his own company of engineers.

When, in 1605, the English Catholic Sir Robert Catesby hatched his plot to murder James I and most of the noblemen of England by blowing up Parliament, he knew that he would need a specialist in the use of gunpowder. The plot also involved kidnapping a minor princess and putting her on the throne to use as a puppet until Spanish troops could arrive, but Catesby thought he could handle that himself. His friend Hugh Owen had fought with the Spanish in the Netherlands and knew Fawkes. A message was sent to Fawkes asking for his help, and so Fawkes came to London.

It was Fawkes who bought and inspected the gunpowder, storing it in cellars under the House of Lords. It was Fawkes who acquired the fuses and tinder needed to set off the blast. And it was Fawkes who volunteered to light the fuses. By 4 November 1605 the Government knew that there was a plot to murder the king at the opening of Parliament the next day, but did not know who would deliver the fatal blow nor when. The guards at Parliament were ordered to search the premises and keep an eye open for anything suspicious.

One of the guards saw Fawkes supposedly retiring to his bedroom to sleep, but taking with him his boots, spurs and riding cloak. Thinking this odd, the man reported the fact. The captain of the guard ordered Fawkes to be arrested and his chambers searched. When the guards arrived, Fawkes had gone but it did not take them long to track him to the cellar that he had rented. There they found him with a lighted match and almost a ton of gunpowder. He was arrested.

Catesby, meanwhile, was putting the rest of his plot into operation assuming that the king and lords would die the next day. The rising proved to be abortive, and the plotters were either killed in the fighting or executed after a short trial. Fawkes himself was hanged in January 1606.

There is no written evidence linking Fawkes to either Church Passage or Stonegate, though he doubtless would have walked along both several times during his early years living in York. It may be only that the ghost wears a hat, cloak and clothes of about the right date that has identified this phantom with Fawkes. The identification does at least perpetuate in spectral form the memory of one of York's most infamous sons.

Glowing Red as Hot Coals: The Barguest of the Snickleways

Church Passage is but one of many narrow alleys and passages that link the main streets of the city. All of them are so narrow that only pedestrians may pass through them, and not a few are wide enough only for one person to pass at a time. They are known collectively as snickleways and together form a network of maze-like complexity running through the ancient city. They are generally thought to be of medieval origin, but probably date back to at least the Viking period.

It is in these narrow thoroughfares that the horrendous Barguest is said to lurk. This supernatural beast is generally said to be ill-disposed toward humans, and some think that it is downright evil. It usually takes the form of a huge black dog, more like a donkey in size, which has a coat of shaggy black hair. Its eyes are the worst aspect of the fearful hound, being as big and round as saucers and glowing as red as hot coals as if with a deep inner fire. It is these eyes that are the mark of the Barguest and by which it may be recognised. Although it is usually said to take the form of a great black hound, the creature may appear in a variety of guises. It has been seen as a calf, as a horse and as a shapeless, shifting, slithering thing.

These days the snickleways are lit by electric light, but in years gone by they had no illumination at all except for that provided by the moon, stars or the traveller's lantern. They must have been dark, eerie places at night, just the sort of area where a supernatural beast might roam. There are numerous stories told about the Barguest and its malevolent actions. It is generally held that if the Barguest pushes past you, then you are safe. But if it stops to look at you with its terrible, fear-inducing eyes then it has fixed upon you as a victim. Death, or at least serious misfortune, will not be far away.

It might be thought that the Barguest of York's snickleways is just the sort of nightmare beast that might be imagined slinking along dark alleys, or that it could be a totally imaginary beast invented by parents to stop their children wandering down the alleyways after dark. But things are not that simple.

The Barguest is but one of a large number of similar beasts that, as tradition and legend have it, may be met across much of England. In East Anglia the supernatural dogs with glowing eyes are known as Shuck, and the name is now widely used by researchers to refer to all such unearthly creatures. They do, however, go by a variety of names. Scarf, Shock, Skeff, Chuff and Rugman are all names applied to this supernatural beast.

Although the Shuck is usually viewed as being the harbinger of evil or misfortune, this is not always so. In Lincolnshire it is thought to be violently aggressive only to evil men, and is held to be particularly friendly toward women. There are numerous tales of women walking alone at night who are escorted by Shuck, which frightens off would-be attackers. The Barguest is firmly of the malevolent variety of Shuck.

The fact that these shape-shifting dogs with red eyes are largely confined to eastern England has led some to believe that whatever Shuck is, it came to England with the Vikings. It was this area of the country that was most heavily settled by the Norsemen and went by the name of the Danelaw. Some have looked to the pagan beliefs of the Vikings for some explanation of the terrible Barguest, Shuck and the like. They did not have far to look.

The pagan myths of the Vikings are filled with hellish hounds of fearsome aspect. The watchman of the giants, Eggther, for instance, had a guard dog named Garm whose howl was deafening. But the hound thought by most folklorists to be linked to Shuck was Fenrir. This gigantic wolf-dog was the embodiment of chaos and destruction and was thought to roam looking for souls to consume. His final battle against the gods would end in his death at the hands of Vidar, the heroic son of Odin, but would presage the coming of Ragnarok, the twilight of the gods when all the world would be destroyed. Of course, there is no way of knowing if the Barguest and Shuck are merely half-forgotten memories of the terrible Fenrir. These powerful and dangerous black dogs may be remaining echoes of some other pagan deity. Or they may really exist and be padding the snickleways of York even as you read this book.

The 'Thing' in Ye Olde Starre Inn

Also in Stonegate is Ye Olde Starre Inn, one of the most welcoming old pubs in the city. There are several different ghost stories about this pub. One tells that wounded Royalist soldiers fleeing from the Battle of Marston Moor in 1644 were brought here by their dashing commander Prince Rupert during the night after the battle. Rupert had to flee with the remnants of his defeated army before he was trapped in the city by the advancing Roundheads, commanded by Sir Thomas Fairfax and Oliver Cromwell. Before he left he paid the landlord to care for the wounded men left here.

In the short but violent siege of York that followed the battle, the pub was used as a makeshift hospital by the defending Cavaliers. Wounded men were brought here for the rudimentary treatment that the doctors of the time could offer. This treatment was often more effective and

The exterior of Ye Olde Starre Inn in Stonegate was used as a hospital during the 1644 siege of York, and the ghosts of wounded soldiers remain.

The phantom cats of Ye Olde Starre Inn are often seen in this ground-floor room.

considerate than some modern books might imply, but it always suffered from one terrible defect: there was no such thing as anaesthetic. Other than a good stiff drink of brandy or port, the unfortunates who were wounded were offered no pain relief. And if their wounds necessitated the amputation of a limb, they would suffer pain so excruciating that it is quite impossible to describe.

One portion of the cellar of Ye Olde Starre was put aside for the use of the surgeons who cut out bullets from living flesh and amputated arms or legs. As can be imagined, the screams of the men subjected to these brutal but life-saving treatments were terrible and piteous to hear. If the stories are true, there might be no need to imagine at all, for the phantom screams of the wounded men are said to be heard here still.

A much more gentle spectre is sometimes seen on the stairs that lead from the bar to the first floor. This ghost takes the form of an elderly lady who is seen walking slowly up the stairs. She is seen only by young children who, understandably, fail to give a clear description of her to the adults who want to know.

In 1644, Prince Rupert, the Royalist commander at the Battle of Marston Moor, lodged his wounded soldiers in Ye Olde Starre Inn before riding off to report on his defeat to Charles I.

The most bizarre phantoms in the pub, however, are the two ghostly black cats that play and scamper around the ground floor. The staff and regulars know that the two felines are phantoms, but tourists and travellers who encounter them will mistake them for real, living pets. More than one person has reached out to stroke them only for their hand to meet nothing but a chilly patch of empty air.

It is not clear which of these ghosts, if any, accounts for the 'thing' in the main bar. No human has ever seen this thing, but there can be little doubt that it is there. It is seen only by dogs. On many occasions a dog has been suddenly awoken from its slumber beside its owner in the bar by some unseen thing. The dog will react as if some hostile person or creature is in the room. It will snarl, growl and stare intently at something that no human can see. The invisible thing may stay still, or it may move slowly around the bar. In the 1980s one dog decided to launch a savage attack on the invisible intruder. With fangs bared and claws foremost it lunged across the bar with a terrifying howl. Unfortunately for the dog it passed straight through whatever it was intending to attack and slammed at full speed into the wall, knocking itself unconscious.

The enclosed snickleway of Mad Alice Lane is haunted by the ghost of the eponymous Mad Alice.

'Mad Alice Lane': Lund Court

Leave Ye Olde Starre Inn and head north-east along Stonegate. At the far end of this street, turn right into Low Petergate. You will soon find Lund Court, also known as Mad Alice Lane, on the right. This narrow alleyway is haunted by the eponymous Mad Alice, a poor lady of early Victorian times who lost her mind.

In search of his own Head: The Phantom of Holy Trinity Churchyard

Continue along Low Petergate to the crossways junction. Turn left into Goodramgate, possibly the most haunted street in England. After a few yards you will find a gateway on your left that gives access to Holy Trinity churchyard. The most frequently seen phantom in this churchyard is that of a lady in a long black dress. She roams among the tombs as if searching for something.

Sometimes she scans the ground, but at other times she will peer at the inscriptions, seeming to look for some name or other. Unfortunately, as is so often the case, nobody is at all certain who this lady might be or for what she searches. The ghost began to be seen, it is thought, about the time of the First World War and it is usually thought that either she or the person whose grave she seeks must have died at that date. But nobody really knows. She is just one of those many ghosts who are pottering around York on business of their own.

Very clearly identified is the other ghost seen in and around the churchyard. This is the phantom of Thomas Percy, 7th Earl of Northumberland, in his time one of the richest and most powerful men in England. But that did not save him from the executioner's axe in 1572. The Percy family enters history in 1066 when a humble knight named William rode out of the village of Percy in Normandy to join the army being gathered by Duke William of Normandy to invade England. This William de Percy fought bravely at the Battle of Hastings, which won William the throne of England, and later performed important duties during the arduous few years of uprisings that followed. William de Percy was rewarded with extensive lands and estates across Yorkshire and Lincolnshire.

In 1315 his descendant Henry Percy was raised to the peerage as Lord Percy of Alnwick. By this date the Percys were a bulwark against the Scots, raising men and money to form armies to drive off marauding Scots coming over the border. In 1377 King Edward III raised the then head of the family to the title of Earl of Northumberland, bestowing even more land

Holy Trinity churchyard is said to be haunted by the ghost of a lady in a long black dress who roams among the tombs as if searching for something.

Thomas Percy, 7th Earl of Northumberland, was one of the richest and most powerful men in England, but he came to a violent end and his phantom now haunts Holy Trinity.

on the family. Thereafter the Percys have been the greatest family of northern England, with a history and lineage that no other family could rival. On more than one occasion a Percy has died leaving only daughters, but always the husband of the eldest daughter has adopted the name of Percy for himself and his offspring to perpetuate the grand family name, and the Percys still hold the Northumberland title. Such was Thomas Percy's proud background.

Thomas Percy did not inherit his family's traditional tact and astute political skills. While everyone else in 1570s England was thankfully turning their backs on religious intolerance and embracing Queen Elizabeth's moderate Protestant fudge in religious matters, Thomas decided to parade his Catholic faith in public. Not only that, but he wrote a series of letters to the equally Catholic Mary Queen of Scots, who was being held in comfortable imprisonment by Elizabeth. There was nothing outwardly improper about the letters that he wrote or received, but they were dangerous. The Pope had ruled that Elizabeth had been born out of wedlock, and if she were illegitimate then the true monarch of England should have been Mary. Therefore, for a Catholic nobleman of huge wealth and power to write to Mary was to court suspicion of treason.

And then in 1579 Thomas Percy went even further. He knew that many people, perhaps the majority, in northern England were not Protestants. Some were still openly Catholic, others merely disapproved of the new religious teachings being propounded in their parish churches. Percy's mistake was to think that this religious feeling would translate into disloyalty to Queen Elizabeth and the Kingdom of England. Together with the equally Catholic Earl of Westmorland, Percy raised a rebellion. He summoned his retainers, tenants and all those who cared for the Catholic faith to join him and Westmorland in an uprising that would see the northern counties secede from Elizabeth's Protestant England. He sent messages to Catholic monarchs abroad asking for men and arms, promising to put Mary on the throne.

In the event, Percy's followers chose to stay at home and help from abroad was too slow in arriving. Percy and Westmorland were reduced to riding around the northern counties with a small band of horsemen and some impressive banners, but no army and still less support. Royal troops hurried north and soon had Percy under lock and key, Westmorland having escaped to France. Thomas Percy remained in prison for three years, too dangerous to release and too powerful to execute.

Then in 1572 the Ridolfi Plot was exposed. This was a plot hatched by the Catholic Duke of Norfolk and an Italian banker named Roberto Ridolfi. The aim of this plot was to use Italian money to hire Catholic mercenaries who would land on Norfolk's estates while a rising of English Catholics was organised. Elizabeth was to be murdered, Mary put on the throne and England forced to embrace Catholicism again. Elizabeth decided it was time for a firm hand. Norfolk and Percy were both condemned to death.

Percy was hauled from his cell to be executed in the open street. His head was then taken to the Micklegate Bar and set up on the wooden spike over the battlements. Every time his old retainers, tenants and relatives came to York they would be forcibly reminded of the penalties of rebellion. The head did not remain there for long. A loyal Percy servant climbed up Micklegate Bar one dark night while a second kept watch. The head was retrieved and taken to the Holy Trinity churchyard for burial in holy ground. It did not stay in the churchyard long either. The second servant proved to be less loyal than the first, and gleefully claimed a reward of 10s 6d for the return of the head to the authorities.

It is this grisly tale that has convinced most researchers that the headless man whose ghost is sometimes seen wandering about the churchyard is the phantom of the luckless Thomas Percy. Presumably he is looking for his head.

Some reports hold that there is a third ghost here, that of a nun or lady in a grey or white gown who is seen in the church itself.

The Happy Ghost Girl of the Snickleway Inn

Not far from Holy Trinity Church is a pub that for centuries was called the Angler's Arms, but which has recently been dubbed the Snickleway Inn. Despite the change in name, the ghost remains. This takes the form of a girl aged about eight or nine years, who trots up and down the staircase. Those who have encountered her say that she seems quite happy and cheerful.

The Snickleway Inn has the ghost of a young girl who runs on the staircase. She is perhaps the most active of all the ghosts in York – according to the landlord.

The Tragic Ghost of Marmaduke's Restaurant

Also in Goodramgate stands Marmaduke's Restaurant, which takes its name from the ghost that haunts it. Marmaduke lived here in the late seventeenth and early eighteenth centuries. He had a tragic life, having been born badly crippled. In those less understanding days, those with physical deformities were not as caringly treated as they are today. If a person could not earn a living they were a burden on their families and did not always fare well. Poor Marmaduke did his best to be helpful about the house, but his family made it clear that they resented the waste of money they spent on food and clothes for him. Eventually in 1715 the unhappy Marmaduke hanged himself in an upstairs room. Before he died the boy scratched into the wall the inscription:

Marmaduke Buckle

1715

1697

17

The numbers are his birth and death dates together with his age.

Strangely, this tragic death does not mean that the spectral Marmaduke has become embittered toward humanity. He does not return to wreak vengeance on the society that caused him so much pain in life. Indeed Marmaduke has continued to be a helpful soul about the place. He will tidy up pencils on desks and put away magazines that have been left lying about.

The Bodies in the Cupboard at Bedern

Other unhappy youngsters haunt the narrow alleyway known as Bedern that runs off Goodramgate. This little street was redeveloped in the later twentieth century, but before that date it was lined by Victorian tenements that had been built in the 1860s on the site of the old workhouse, known formally as the York Industrial Ragged School. This was an establishment for orphans or children of impoverished parents who could not afford to keep them. In theory the children were given a roof over their heads, adequate food and training in some skill that would help them to earn a living when, as teenagers, they were turned out to make their way in the world.

The theory was good, but it depended very largely on the honesty and hard work of the man appointed by the city authorities to run the place. Between 1847 and 1855 this establishment was in the hands of a drunk who neglected his duties and handed out savage beatings to any child who complained. Like many drunks, he could be charming and apparently sober when he wanted and so managed to fool the authorities for a long time. It was only when dark rumours began to circulate that he was investigated and sacked.

Quite how bad the man's regime was is a matter of conjecture. The worst that was proved against him was that he had given overly vicious beatings to children and had pilfered city funds to pay for his drinking and gambling. However, gossip had it that he had beaten to death more than one child. The bodies were, it was said, hidden in a large cupboard in his room until he could get hold of the only undertaker he could bribe to cover up the bruising and other injuries. Some said that bodies still lay hidden somewhere in the building after he was dismissed, but if so they were never found.

After the institution was moved to improved premises and given a more trustworthy chief, the old buildings were torn down and replaced by housing which survived for a century before they too were demolished. As has become usual in central York, the cleared site was handed over to archaeologists to perform an emergency excavation before the builders moved in. Several of those working on the site felt unaccountably uneasy, as if they were being watched. One man had a particularly unnerving experience. He was busy on the dig when he felt somebody tap him urgently and insistently on the shoulder, but when he turned around there was nobody there. When he undressed that evening his wife told him to look at his back in the mirror.

The rather ominous archway that gives access to the courtyard of Bedern, off Goodramgate. This little street has a grim history, and is now the denizen of sad spectres.

On the shoulder where he had felt the taps were parallel bruises as if he had been gripped hard by the fingers of a child-sized hand.

There have been other incidents since the old houses were pulled down. Several people walking past late at night, when the city is quiet and still, have heard the sounds of laughing and singing children coming from the side street. One person felt an invisible child's hand slipped into his as he passed by, as if the child were seeking the reassurance of a friendly adult.

The Jovial Ghosts of the Old White Swan

Also in Goodramgate is the Old White Swan pub. This is a rambling old pub that actually occupies what were originally four houses grouped around a courtyard, which accounts for the odd changes in floor and ceiling level from one room to the next. One of the downstairs rooms has an old fireplace, and this is the focus of the haunting. The ghosts manifest themselves only in the winter when a fire blazes in the fireplace. Then a group of four gentlemen in colourful waistcoats and riding breeches will materialise, grouped around the flames as if warming

The Old White Swan in Goodramgate is a rambling old pub, which has a haunted fireplace.

themselves after a long ride through the chilly winter air. Everyone who has seen them reports that these are jovial ghosts indeed. Laughing and joking, the phantoms seem to be having a thoroughly good time.

'This is Our House Now, Not Yours': The Rude Ghost of Colliergate

At the end of Goodramgate, but before reaching the city walls, turn right into Aldwark, then take the first right into St Andrewgate and so back to crossways junction. Look left down Colliergate to see the shops that line both sides. One of these shops – the owner has asked for anonymity – had a rather unpleasant ghost on the first floor.

This ghost took the form of a shortish elderly man dressed in tailcoat and tight riding breeches that seem to date him to the early nineteenth century. Just such a man had died here in the 1840s, after living in what was then a house for some decades. The old man was a recluse who kept pretty much to himself except when out on business. He never invited guests to his house to dine, and allowed only his servants over the threshold. He was well known not to like women, there was talk of an unhappy romance in his youth, and never employed any female staff.

After the man's death, his phantom was seen on the first floor where he had lived. He seems to have appeared most often when women were in the house, and gave out a most determined air of belligerence and hostility.

In the 1970s the shop came into the hands of two women, and this seems to have prompted the ghost into a bout of great activity. Presumably not having allowed women into his house when alive he did not want them there when he was dead. The two women were understandably disturbed by the frequent appearances of a hostile phantom. On one occasion, when one of the women was walking up the stairs to the first floor, she saw the ghost waiting for her on the landing with his habitual look of dislike on his face. The woman had had enough.

'I will not leave,' she declared in a firm voice. 'This is our house now, not yours.' The ghost looked at her in surprise, then vanished. He was not seen again so long as the ladies had the lease of the shop.

The Crushing of the Pearl of York: The Shrine of St Margaret Clitherow

Cross over Colliergate and then bear left into Shambles. In this busy, bustling street is a small haven of peace in the form of the Shrine of St Margaret Clitherow, often known as the Pearl of York. After the rebellion led by Westmorland and Percy, and the unmasking of the Ridolfi Plot, the government of Elizabeth I decided to crack down on Catholics who preferred to put their allegiance to the Pope in Rome than the Queen of England. Although Catholics were not persecuted as such, priests were banned from entering England from abroad on pain of death and anyone who gave them lodgings was under immediate suspicion of treason. The Catholic monarchs abroad did, indeed, seek to send assassins to murder Elizabeth and several priests were charged with discovering if the English were ready for a religious rebellion. The intrigues would reach their peak in 1588 when King Philip II of Spain sent the Armada of ships and soldiers to invade England and so impose Catholicism by force. This was a dangerous time to be a Catholic without ostentatiously making demonstrations of loyalty to the English monarchy.

Margaret Clitherow was one who fell foul of the increasingly tense situation. She was born in 1556, the daughter of Thomas Middleton, Sheriff of York, and married John Clitherow, a wealthy butcher who served as chamberlain of the city. She was a Catholic, though her husband was a Protestant, and for some years there was no trouble. However, her brother was a Catholic priest who trained abroad and was, therefore, banned from entering England. When he secretly came to York, Margaret provided him with lodgings and constructed a 'priest's hole' in a property she owned. When the brother moved on, other illegal priests came to stay. Margaret was putting her life at risk, but believed that she owed it to her fellow Catholics to provide accommodation for visiting priests. It was not an unusual situation. Most priests were concerned only with the souls of their spiritual flock, and Catholics such as Margaret Clitherow could see no harm in looking after them. The government, however, was more concerned with the minority of priests who were assassins or spies.

The Shrine of St Margaret Clitherow in Shambles commemorates a resident of York who was canonised and who may haunt the house.

It was on 10 March 1586 that the authorities came and arrested Margaret. One of the priests who she had harboured had been caught and had, apparently, named her as the person who had given him lodgings when he was in York. Margaret refused to plead either guilty or not guilty, and was therefore sent to torture to extract her cooperation with the court. The usual torture for a woman under such circumstances was 'pressing'. This involved being laid flat on the ground and having a door or plank of wood placed across the torso. Increasingly heavy weights were then put on top of the door to slowly crush the unfortunate victim. The attending magistrate urged her again and again to plead her answer to the charges but Margaret refused, declaring that she was suffering for the sake of Jesus. After fifteen minutes of this, Margaret Clitherow died.

The Catholics of the time declared that Margaret had died for her faith and made her a martyr. In 1970 she was canonized as a saint and her old home in Shambles turned into a shrine. Perhaps inevitably, the rather vague wraith seen here is identified as that of St Margaret.

The much haunted Church of St Crux in the Shambles has long since been demolished, but its church hall remains and the ghosts, it is said, walk here still.

The Handsome Phantom at the Church of St Crux

Another religious building used to stand in Shambles, but was demolished in 1887. This was the Church of St Crux, which stood toward the southern end of the street. If you look carefully you can see portions of the walls still standing, built into other structures. The most active of the ghosts which formerly haunted this church was the tall, handsome man who would be seen on many mornings peering out of one the windows that looking on to Shambles. The man was described as having a calm and serene expression, taking no notice of the early morning bustle in the street outside. Some of the bolder passers-by who saw him would call out or wave, but the ghost always ignored them. On one occasion the verger offered to unlock the church early so that folk could go into the church to accost the phantom directly. There were no volunteers.

Like St Crux Church, the Waits of York have now disappeared from the city. For centuries the procession of the Waits patrolled the street at night. This took the form of four burly men dressed in a bold scarlet uniform with embroidered silver badges. Their task was to march the streets at night to keep an eye open for any criminal activity, cry out the hours and watch for indications of what sort of weather awaited the citizens of York the following day. Each man was paid £4 a year for performing his duties. This may not sound like much but when the Waits were instituted this was slightly higher than the average worker received – and no labourer got a smart uniform or the respect that went with it. Only later when inflation got a grip did the salary become unattractive.

To pass the time on their endless nightly rambles through the streets, some Waits got into the habit of singing or playing musical instruments. It was this that attracted the second ghost of St Crux, for she appeared only when the Waits were singing. As the men paced past St Crux the figure of a beautiful young woman dressed in a long pale gown – some said it was her winding sheet – would slip out of the churchyard. She would follow the Waits pace by pace, stopping when they did, then following again when they resumed their march. If one of the men boldly went back to approach her, she would vanish. The ghost's favourite route was along Pavement, then up Colliergate and into Goodramgate where she would fade from view.

Some believe that this lady phantom is identical to the third ghost of St Crux, though other researchers think that they are distinct entities. In any case, this third spectre is still seen from time to time even though the church is gone. She takes the form of a lady in a flowing gown wearing a veil or shawl over her head. She walks from the site of the demolished church along Pavement and into Stonebow, then along Peasholme Green to reach the Foss Bridge where she always vanishes.

Yet another ghostly woman, or again perhaps the same one, walks from the site of St Crux to Spen Lane. There she pauses a moment before vanishing. Whether these are all the same ghost or different ones is difficult to determine. The few witnesses who have seen the phantoms that walk to Foss Bridge or Spen Lane are unable to give a clear description of the ghostly ladies. They say the ghosts are female and wear long gowns or dresses, but that is about it. Unless a clear description can ever be obtained the identification of these almost identical ghosts must remain a mystery.

There was one witness to an appearance of a ghost at St Crux whose powers of observation must surely be trusted; he was a policeman on patrol. This experience took place when the church was standing empty immediately before its demolition. The policeman, taking the place of the vanished Waits, was on patrol in the early hours of the morning when he came plodding down Shambles. Hearing organ music coming from the abandoned church, the policeman was puzzled. Thinking that some prankster might have broken into the church, he decided to investigate. As he came up to the church he noticed that the organ was playing a tune then popular at funerals.

The policeman had got to about three yards from the doors when the music stopped. The locked doors then flew open revealing the dark, empty interior of the church. But the church was not entirely empty. The by now thoroughly scared policemen could hear the sounds of footsteps and muttered voices as if a congregation were leaving after a service. Not surprisingly he took to his heels and fled. When the policeman summoned up the courage to return with a colleague, they found that the church was silent and the doors firmly locked.

A Mysterious Obsession at All Saints' Church

At the southern end of Shambles, turn right into Pavement to find All Saints' Church, which is still standing. The ghost here has the peculiar habit of appearing only when a funeral service is taking place. Her behaviour is always the same. At some point in the service she will appear

All Saints' Church in Pavement has a ghost that appears only when a funeral service is taking place.

near the door of the church to gaze intently at the coffin. If she is approached she will invariably vanish, but otherwise will remain for some time. One person at a service watched her for more than five minutes before she faded from view.

This ghost is usually described as being that of a young woman with dark hair, which tumbles in carefully dressed curls down to her waist. Opinions differ among witnesses as to her dress, but it is usually said to be fairly plain and long. There is, sadly, no story attached to this spectre. This is a shame for her obsession with funerals must surely point to some sort of clear link. Perhaps she died in circumstances that meant she could not be given a Christian burial, or maybe she had wanted to be buried here, but was interred elsewhere.

The Seven Ghosts of the Golden Fleece Pub

There is, however, a very clear story about the ghost at the Golden Fleece pub, also in Pavement.

The sign of the Golden Fleece marks a pub with a remarkably active set of ghosts.

The pub dates back to 1503 and serves hearty hot meals daily, while offering five real ales and a full range of drinks. During the later years of the Second World War, Yorkshire was the home county for dozens of squadrons of RAF Bomber Command. The county offered plenty of flat, open country on which large airbases could be built and the ground was generally firm enough to take the weight of the big, four-engined bombers that were taking off on most nights to pound the war industries of the Third Reich. This was dangerous work, with Bomber Command crews sustaining the highest casualty rates of any force during the war. A man who served as part of a bomber aircrew had only a 50 per cent chance of getting through the war without being killed or injured.

By February 1944 the Yorkshire airfields had been allocated to 6 Group, equipped with Lancaster and Halifax bombers. Although 6 Group was officially part of RAF Bomber Command, it was in fact an arm of the Royal Canadian Air Force, being crewed entirely by Canadians, and most ground staff came from across the Atlantic as well. It is often forgotten just how great a contribution Canada made to the British war effort. Despite the fact that by 1939 Canada was an independent nation, albeit sharing the same monarch as Britain, she came into the war on 10 September 1939. Although she had a population only a quarter that of Britain, Canada sent hundreds of thousands of men to fight, all of them volunteers. Conscripts were called up, but were put to work on reserve duties to free the volunteers for the war. In all 41,000 Canadians were killed and another 54,000 wounded before peace came in 1945.

The bomber squadrons based in Yorkshire were among the elite of the Canadian war effort. The complex instrumentation and machinery involved with bombers meant that only men of above average education and intelligence were accepted into the force. These men risked

The stone-flagged alley outside the Golden Fleece pub, where the ghost of a man in uniform is sometimes seen.

their lives every time they took off, and had to study hard in between missions to improve their chances of survival. It is no wonder that when they were off duty they chose to enjoy themselves in noisy and boisterous fashion. As the nearest city of any size, York played host to the Canadian airmen on their nights off.

It is one of these gallant, hard-drinking Canadians named Monroe who haunts the Golden Fleece. During some drunken larking about, this airman fell out of a first-floor window and broke his neck on the stone pavement outside. He died instantly. The airman is still seen from time to time in his RCAF uniform in the bedroom from which he fell and also, though not so often, in the street outside.

An American tourist, April Keenan, encountered the ghostly airman in 1994. She saw him quite distinctly in her bedroom when she awoke in the small hours of the morning. The ghost

The main bar of the Golden Fleece pub is home to the spectre of a young boy who died here after a road accident.

was standing looking out of the fatal window. Thinking she had an intruder in her room, Ms Keenan cried out in alarm. When the figure took no notice of her, she boldly got out of bed to shake him by the arm and demand what he was doing in her room. Her hand met only empty air and the apparition vanished abruptly.

He is not the only ghost here. The Golden Fleece has no less than seven ghosts and claims that its phantoms are the most active in York. In the two downstairs bars there is the spectre of a young boy who was trampled by a horse in the days when this was a coaching inn. The unfortunate child was carried into the bar, but died within minutes. Customers sometimes feel him trying to pick their pockets. There is also a highwayman who is named 'One-Eyed Jack'. He has been seen throughout the pub.

Several of the upstairs rooms have their own particular ghosts. In the Minster Suite bedroom the bed has moved and children's crying has been heard. In the Shambles bedroom people have had the sensation of a figure sitting on the bed and strange lights being observed. In 2008 a pair of guests left after seeing a candle stick move along the fireplace with a dark shape at the side of it. Their unease can be gauged by the fact that they left without asking for the return of the money that they had paid in advance when booking the room. In St Catherine's room dark figures have been recorded and this is the room Yvette Fielding, from the *Most Haunted* television programme,

Lady Alice Peckett died three centuries ago, but her ghost still haunts the Meadery Room at the Golden Fleece pub.

heard a ghostly laugh that was recorded on her microphone. In Lady Peckett's room the lady herself has been seen and she has been seen on the stairwell. This is Lady Alice Peckett, wife of Sir John Peckett, Lord Mayor of York in 1702. The couple owned the section of the pub, then a separate house, which now forms the yard at the rear and adjoining structures. The phantom of the late Lady Peckett is one of the more active in the pub. She is seen most often around midnight and in the hours that follow. She is seen often in the Meadery Room – a function room available for hire to anyone who fancies having a ghost join their party.

In the downstairs function room a lady has been seen running through the wall screaming as if being chased. There is also the phantom of a dog – a spectre that is usually explained by the fact that years ago workmen lifted the floorboards and found a skeleton of a small dog. In past centuries it was not unusual for the body of an animal to be buried in the foundations of an important new building, so such grisly finds are not as rare as might be expected. Pagan customs die hard.

'She Emanated a feeling of Evil': Coppergate Shopping Centre

At the south-western end of Pavement there is a junction with Parliament Street, coming down from the north. Continue straight on into Coppergate, passing the modern Coppergate Shopping Centre on the left.

In the later nineteenth century, a rather unpleasant old woman lived in one of the houses demolished to make way for the shopping centre. Fate had not been kind to her, for her husband had died young and she was childless. Despite her good looks and the wealth inherited from her husband, the woman made no effort to find a new husband, and none of the York citizens who met her had been tempted in any case. The woman was bad tempered and vindictive. Her enmity was easily earned, for she was a miser of avaricious habits always on the look out for a way to cheat tradesmen or neighbours. Anyone who caught her out would be marked down as a target for her malicious tongue to spread ugly rumours, and for even more vindictive attempts at spiteful tricks. Unsurprisingly it was not long before she alienated all her friends, so she lived alone in the house, apart from servants who rarely stayed very long. She was widely believed to have stashed most of her wealth, in the form of golden sovereigns, somewhere in the house.

Late one night passers-by heard her calling and screaming from an upstairs window. Fearing that thieves were inside in search of her rumoured golden wealth, neighbours broke the door down and rushed upstairs. They found the woman alone in bed raving and muttering. She declared that she had been visited by the ghost of her husband and others who had urged her to repent and pay back those she had cheated. In front of her aghast neighbours, the woman cackled and swore, declaring that the people had deserved to be cheated and that she would never repent. A seizure then struck the woman and she collapsed into a coma.

A doctor was summoned, but there was nothing he could do. The woman died before dawn. The woman's relatives were informed and they came to settle her affairs. No great store of sovereigns was ever found, only the sort of silver coins that a woman might expect to have around the house.

Thereafter the house was haunted by the wicked old woman's ghost. She was seen most often in the upstairs room where she had died, but sometimes in a downstairs room. She always had a vindictive look on her face and some reported that she emanated a feeling of evil. Some thought that the ghost's presence in the downstairs room might be a clue as to the whereabouts of her fabled wealth, but no amount of searching turned up a hidden pot of gold. When the house was demolished and the site cleared there was still no sign of the gold. Perhaps it never existed.

The ghost would seem to have gone too. As so often, building works seem to have had a profound effect on the ghostly inhabitants. Some works will start a haunting, others will end one, and that was also the case here. The ghost has not been seen since the house went.

Poltergeist Attack! Mysterious Fire Alarm Pranks at Coppergate Walk

Running off the south side of Coppergate is the narrow walkway of Coppergate Walk, which leads to the Jorvik Centre where Viking York is recreated for tourists. The shops on the right of the alley were built in the 1980s on the site of what had been the old Craven's Sweet factory. In the 1990s shop No. 8 suffered a dramatic poltergeist attack, which put it into the news headlines. The favourite trick of the mysterious entity was to set off the fire alarms in these buildings with monotonous regularity. In addition the poltergeist exhibited all the usual stunts of such a paranormal visitor. The place was plagued by repeated bangs and raps from no obvious source, things went missing or were moved about and some objects appeared from nowhere.

Castlegate has two female ghosts that frequent its pavements.

To find another scene of poltergeist activity, return to Coppergate and head toward the River Ouse. Turn right just before the bridge to enter Coney Street. In the 1950s a jeweller's shop in this street suffered another news-worthy poltergeist attack.

Tinkling in the Snickleway, Judge's Court

Just off Coney Street runs the snickleway of Judge's Court, where a ghostly man heralds his imminent appearance in a most unusual fashion. In the few seconds before he manifests himself visibly, this ghost emits a soft tinkling sound as if a small metal chain is being dragged over the pavement here. The figure of a large man wearing a heavy overcoat or cloak of some kind then gradually appears. The man is seen to stand in a corner of the snickleway, before he fades away again.

This is one of the most active ghosts in the City of York, being reported several times each year. He even appeared when a tourist guide was escorting a group of foreign tourists around the city and paused here to point out a feature of historic interest. The guide was struck momentarily dumb by the apparition, but then managed to get on with his story. The ghost, on that occasion, was seen by several of the tourists as well as by the guide.

Although the ghost's identity is unknown, his history is not a total mystery, and neither is the strange tinkling sound. In the 1960s some renovations were being undertaken to one of the houses that overlook Judge's Court. An old, sealed-up well was found under the kitchen floor and it was investigated. At the bottom lay the skeleton of a large, burly man. The unfortunate man was still wearing the remnants of a pair of tough riding boots, complete with spurs. But one of the spurs was broken in such a way that the dangling metal would have made a tinkling noise as the man walked.

Ness Hall

Return to Coney Street and head back to Coppergate. Cross straight over the junction to enter the small open space that is Ness Square. Here you will find Ness Hall, which is allegedly haunted.

The Phantom Quaker of Castlegate House

Continue across Ness Square, then bear left into Castlegate. This short street has two ghosts that frequent its pavements. The first is one of those ladies in grey who haunt so many parts of England. This ghost is usually said to be a phantom Quaker and is usually encountered outside Castlegate House, or sometimes inside it. The second ghost is also a lady, though apparently she is distinct from the female phantom of Castlegate House. This spectre is to be seen at No. 6.

The Phantom in Search of its own Body at St Mary's Church

A little further along Castlegate stands St Mary's Church, the churchyard of which is haunted by the phantom of a man who committed among the most gruesome and infamous murders of the early seventeenth century. Walter Calverley was born into a relatively prosperous Yorkshire family of gentlemen farmers in the later sixteenth century. Although the Calverleys were Catholics, they did not parade their faith and so remained largely out of the eye of the authorities. In 1599, Walter married Phillipa Brooke, an heiress from the south of England and took up residence in the family home of Calverley Hall near Leeds.

Calverley was soon in trouble of some kind, the records are not clear quite what, and was fined by the magistrates. A few months later he was in prison and soon afterwards was being pursued through the courts for large unpaid debts. In early 1605 three events happened in the Calverley family that seemed to affect Walter badly. First, Phillipa gave birth to a third son. Second, Walter's mother Katherine changed her will so that her impressive estates and vast wealth would pass not to her son Walter, but to her three grandsons with Phillipa as the trustee. Third, a new court action for unpaid debts was launched against Walter by neighbours.

Something seemed to snap in Walter's mind. He became noticeably morose and truculent. He took to riding alone around the Yorkshire countryside, ignoring his friends and relations.

On 5 April he returned from one such ride to Calverley Hall. Striding into the house he came across his eldest son playing with a spinning top in the entrance hall. Walter drew the knife and stabbed the boy dead. He then strode to his wife's chamber and stabbed her before turning on the middle son and slitting his throat.

Phillipa's maid came in at that point, saw the bloody scene and screamed. Walter attacked her, but the screams brought in two manservants who fought him off. Walter then ran out of the house and remounted his horse. He rode off in the direction of the nearby village where his youngest son was with his wet nurse. Guessing his murderous intentions toward the babe in arms, one of the servants gave chase riding bareback on another horse grabbed hurriedly from the stables. The dramatic life or death chase ended when the servant caught up with Walter as he was trying to batter in the door of the wet nurse's house. The young woman had locked the door on seeing Walter approaching with a drawn knife. There then followed a struggle as the servant summoned villagers to his aid and Walter was overpowered.

Walter refused to give any explanation of his actions. When he was brought to trial at the York Assizes he said nothing in his own defence, refused to hire a lawyer and listened without emotion to the evidence. Today he would almost certainly be diagnosed as insane, but in that less understanding age he was executed.

The case caused a sensation, with a pamphlet being printed and reprinted both in York and London. A play based on the case was staged in London even before the trial, being updated to include the execution once that had taken place. The story spread overseas and featured in newsheets in France and the Netherlands.

Amazingly Phillipa survived the attack. She remarried, bearing her second husband three daughters. The baby son, Henry, lived until 1652 and his son, another Walter, married a rich heiress and was raised to the minor nobility.

After the execution, Walter's body was taken to St Mary's for burial. Even a man guilty of such a hideous crime was deemed worthy of God's grace. What happened to the body next is confused. The parish records are quite clear that it was buried, and contain no records of an exhumation. His tomb, however, is at Calverley and tradition has it that the murderer's bones were moved a few years after the execution.

It is thought to be for this reason that the ghost of Walter Calverley wanders around the churchyard of St Mary's. The phantom, it is said, is searching for its corporeal body. It searches in vain, of course, for it is no longer there.

A Hypnotic Reincarnation of the Massacre at St Mary's Church

St Mary's Church acquired fame outside of York when it became the focus for a most peculiar supernatural mystery in the 1970s. The origins of the mystery are to be found more than eight centuries ago and thousands of miles to the east.

On 4 July 1187 the Muslim leader Saladin fought a battle against the Christian Crusaders on the slopes of a hill called the Horns of Hattin. This was no normal victory, for the defeated Christian army was wiped out almost to a man. Those who were not killed were captured and sold into slavery. Among the dead were the Bishop of Acre and the Grand Master of the Knights Templar along with most of his knights. Any of the knights who survived the fighting were stripped of their arms and armour, then handed over to the Islamic mullahs for execution. King Guy of Jerusalem was captured as was the Marquis de Montferrat, perhaps the ablest Christian soldier in the Holy Land, and the Bishop of Lydda. The main portion of the True Cross on which Jesus Christ had been crucified was lost with the Bishop of Lydda. It is thought that Saladin had it destroyed, it has certainly never been seen again. Virtually the entire armed force of the Christians in the Holy Land had been exterminated.

As if that were not bad enough, Saladin capitalised on his victory by capturing the fortress-cities of Acre and Jaffa, then he made a point of marching into Nazareth, birthplace of Christ and trampling the ground beneath the feet of his Muslim soldiers. Saladin then marched on the Holy City of Jerusalem itself. There then followed a savage month-long siege that ended when the Christian commander, Balian of Ibelin, asked for terms. Saladin offered the defenders their lives, but as slaves. Balian responded by saying that he would therefore destroy everything in Jerusalem. He would burn every building, murder the 5,000 Muslims in the city, melt down all money and jewellery and pour it down the drains. Finally, he promised that he and everyone in Jerusalem, even women and children, would fight to the death, promising to kill at least 10,000 of Saladin's men in doing so. Saladin believed Balian, and ordered that the defenders and population of Jerusalem should be allowed to leave alive and unmolested, as long as each person paid a small ransom.

As the fleeing refugees spread the news of the fall of Jerusalem, anger gripped Christendom. Kings and dukes, earls and barons sharpened their swords for holy war. Knights mortgaged their estates to pay for arms, armour and transport to the Holy Land. Muslim traders were butchered without mercy.

There were no Muslims in York, but the citizens were transformed into a mob by their fury when the news reached the city that Jerusalem had fallen. They turned on the only non-Christians they could find, the Jews. For some months the hatred of the Jews grew and festered. There were outbreaks of violence and many citizens refused to have business dealings with the Jews. Then, in 1190, the unrest broke out into violence on a grand scale. A friar arrived in York preaching a new Crusade that was even then mustering under the command of Richard the Lionheart of England. The friar appealed for volunteers and for funds. The people of York gave both willingly, then the turned their eyes on the Jews. They demanded that the Jews, as subjects of King Richard, should pay their fair share toward the costs of the Crusade. The Jews, seeing no reason to pay for a war between Christians and Muslims, declined.

A local man named Richard Malebisse then leapt to the fore. He made an impassioned speech to the citizens declaring that if the Jews would not pay willingly, they should be forced to pay. His demands stirred up the mob, which soon began smashing their way into Jewish shops and Jewish homes to loot them of money. The terrified Jewish population, about 1,500 in all, turned to the only man they thought that they could trust: the Royal Constable of York Castle. King Richard was known to be friendly toward the Jews and had promised them his protection. The constable agreed to give the Jews shelter in the castle, but said he could do nothing to save their houses, shops and property.

The rioting spread through the city and the next morning the mob, led by the friar and Malebisse, appeared at the gates of the castle. When the constable refused them entry, they attacked. The friar was killed, but this only served to inflame the mob even more. Worryingly, the constable soon realised that his own men were not very keen on the fight. Some deserted, others held back from the fray. Clearly they did not want to fight their fellow Christians to save the Jews. The constable advised the Jews to take shelter in the strongest and most formidable portion of the castle, telling them that they had to look to their own safety.

The stronghold to which the Jews withdrew was the keep of the castle which stood isolated on a massive mound of earth at one end of the courtyard. Once the Jews were all inside, the constable opened the castle gates to the mob and ordered his men to stand back. The Jews sent out a messenger offering to pay twice their share to the Crusade in return for safety, but Malebisse killed the messenger and roared out that all the Jews would die. There then followed some hours of desperate fighting, but the Jews realised they could not hold out for long and that no help was within reach. They decided to commit mass suicide, as had other Jewish garrisons throughout the history of their people. Fathers killed their families, then went to the Rabbi to have their throats slit. The Rabbi was last to die.

It was a terrible event, and one which has never been forgotten. But its link to St Mary's Church did not come until the late 1960s when the British hypnotherapist Arnall Bloxham began a series of experiments. Bloxham specialised in regressing patients to see if events in their past could explain emotional problems that they were experiencing. Following procedures developed in the USA, he then began regressing people back to before they were born to uncover what became known as 'past lives'.

Whether or not these actually were previous lives lived by the person is controversial. Many psychologists thought that they might be fantasies developed by the patient to externalise internal problems. Others thought that they were proof of reincarnation.

Clifford's Tower, the ancient keep of York Castle, was the scene of an appalling massacre that has left an indelible spectral mark on the building.

One of Bloxham's patients claimed to have lived before as a young Jewish woman named Rebecca who had been killed in the York riots. The story that she recounted over several hypnotic sessions was long, detailed and accurate. Details of everyday life were recounted with startling clarity and, according to historians, great accuracy. There was, however, one detail that did not ring true. According to 'Rebecca' she and her family had taken refuge not in the castle but in a crypt under the nave of St Mary's Church. 'Rebecca' gave a detailed description of the crypt, and a harrowing account of what happened when the mob broke in to slaughter her and her family. So far as was known all the Jews had gone to the castle, and none were known to have hidden anywhere else. Not only that, but there was no crypt at St Mary's. Most people dismissed the story as the result of her imagination.

Then in 1975 some building works were undertaken at St Mary's. These involved lifting a section of floor in the nave. This revealed a flight of steps which led down to a long-disused crypt that matched the one described by 'Rebecca' almost exactly. It was uncanny, but does it prove that reincarnation happens?

The Glistening Hue of the Phantom Blood at Clifford's Tower

Continue past the church to the end of Castlegate and emerge into the great open space which is now dominated by the huge earthen mound on which stands the stone mass of Clifford's Tower. This is the site of the castle keep to which the Jews fled during the riots of 1190, and where they perished. The original keep was destroyed by fire during the riots, and what stands here today is the structure that was built to replace it. One curious feature of the Tower is that the walls will periodically glisten with a reddish hue. This is traditionally said to be the phantom blood of the Jews who perished here. Scientists think that it is more likely to be a fungus.

'Your Money or Your Life!': The Highwayman of St George's Field

Pass Clifford's Tower to the right and walk south along Tower Street. On your right you will see a tree-shaded stretch of grass known as St George's Field. In centuries past this patch of land formed part of a much larger meadow that filled the area outside the city walls and between the Foss stream and the River Ouse. Much of the area is now covered by a car park but, before the land was properly drained in the early twentieth century, it tended to be boggy and marshy throughout the winter and muddy even in the summer after rain. It flooded often and was never built upon. It made a convenient meeting place for duellists, lovers and others who wanted to be away from prying eyes within the city.

It floods still, though not so often, and the City Council has deemed it useful for nothing except being covered in asphalt to serve as a car park. Maybe they are right. The ghosts, however, have another use for it.

So far as the phantoms are concerned, St George's Field is still an open meadow dotted with trees. They come back time and again, going about their own business and ignoring the humans and their motorised contraptions that dominate the scene today.

Perhaps the most gruesome of York's many ghosts is to be encountered on the grass of St George's Field.

The first of the ghosts here is a gruesome, but unusual figure. This is Baron Stafford, who came from one of the oldest and proudest families in England. The family descends from a minor Norman knight who fought at the Battle of Hastings with William the Conqueror and was granted Stafford Castle and surrounding lands by way of thanks. Over the centuries the family has been promoted through the ranks of nobility to earls, dukes or marquises, lost their titles through rebellion, rebuilt their fortunes, passed the titles through the female line, lost titles again, regained them and gone through periods of penury and affluence. Through all this, however, they have managed to hang on to both Stafford Castle and the title of Baron Stafford – a quite remarkable feat.

In 1694 one of these Staffords came to York on business, but got into a quarrel with a local gentleman. The details of the argument have been lost, but they were considered serious enough by the two men to be the cause of a duel. At this date the duel was, officially at least, illegal in England. In earlier centuries the duel had been considered a better option than a blood feud which might claim the lives of dozens, but there had been too many scandals for it to survive. More than once a highly skilled swordsman had challenged a man with less ability over a mere trifle with the intent of murdering him, and there had also been instances of seconds tampering with guns. By the 1690s a duel between consenting adults of approximately equal ability was unlikely to attract the attentions of the magistrates, but anyone duelling still risked a charge of attempted murder. That was why the Stafford's duel was fought on St George's Field at dawn.

A highwayman haunts St George's Field.

The fight was short and fatal. Stafford received a rapier thrust through the chest just minutes into the fight. He could not believe it, staring in bewilderment at the spreading bloodstain on his shirt before he dropped to the ground. He was dead in seconds.

It is this fatal duel that is replayed time and again in spectral form on St George's Field as the cold light of dawn creeps up over the city. What makes this haunting so peculiar is that only Stafford is seen, the other participants in the duel have not returned. So the ghost of the nobleman is seen apparently dancing around thrusting his sword at some invisible opponent, parrying non-existent thrusts and finally receiving his death wound from a weapon that none can see but himself. As in the real duel the phantom Stafford stares for a moment at the wound, then collapses. And then the ghost vanishes.

The second ghost of St George's Field is that of a man who came from far less exalted stock than Stafford, but who is far better known: Dick Turpin. Turpin was born in Essex in 1706 and apprenticed to a butcher, but he turned bad at a young age and when only a teenager was buying stolen cattle at a cheap price, then passing them on to his master at a profit. When this was discovered he was dismissed and took to burglary. By the age of twenty-one he was leading a tough and merciless gang who specialised in breaking into isolated farms and torturing the inhabitants into revealing the whereabouts of any valuables.

At the age of twenty-five, Turpin made a career change that would ensure his fame when he became a highwayman. In the 1730s the highwaymen were the noblemen of crime, and with good reason. They were looked up to by other criminals, respected by the public and feared by the forces of law and order. Those who became 'gentlemen of the road' knew that to gain the respect of their fellows, the favours of ladies of easy virtue and the wealth they craved, they had to behave in the way highwaymen were expected.

The highwayman was a uniquely English type of criminal. He had first entered the scene in the 1640s when several well-born gentlemen were driven to robbery by circumstance. Those who had joined the Royalist cause had their property confiscated by a vindictively victorious Parliament, and those who joined the rebellion of the youthful Charles II that ended at the Battle of Worcester in 1651 were condemned to death as traitors even before they were arrested and tried.

One such royalist was Captain James Hind who found himself penniless and marked out for death. He had only his horse, his sword, his pistol and the clothes he rode in. Fortunately for Hind, he had a magnificent charger and the fine clothes of a gentleman. When he took to crime the ruffians with whom he mixed could scarcely believe their eyes, nor could many victims who took Hind for the gentleman he was and were aghast when he produced his pistol and demanded, 'your money or your life.' Hind once stopped a coach that contained none other than Oliver Cromwell, but the other occupants of the coach turned out to be well armed, so Hind fled empty handed. When he was eventually captured, Hind was executed for treason and not for his many robberies.

The pattern set by Hind as well as other poverty-stricken cavaliers such as Captain Philip Strafford, Zachary Howard and John Cottington (a Catholic who made a speciality of discussing theology with any Puritan preacher that he robbed) was soon followed by low-born criminals who craved the respect of their social betters. By 1700 most highwaymen still dressed in the finest clothes and rode expensive horses, but none of them had been born gentlemen. Turpin was typical in that he made the change to being a highwayman as a conscious decision to raise his social status among the criminal fraternity.

However, by Turpin's time the open road was becoming a much safer place for travellers than it had formerly been. Town and city authorities no longer restricted their watch or town guards to operating within the city walls. The merchants in cities such as York began to realise that the profitability of their trade depended on customers being able to reach and leave the city safely. Determined efforts were made to patrol the highways and to track down and catch any highwaymen who operated on them.

For six years Turpin got away with his career of crime, but then his safe hideout in a cave in Epping Forest was discovered and he had to go on the run. In 1735 he joined forces with the then rather more notorious highwayman Tom King. This partnership ended when the two men were ambushed at the Green Man in Epping. Turpin opened fire, but accidentally shot King dead before he fled. His movements after this are not known for certain, but in 1738 he came to York using the name of John Palmer, Palmer being his wife's maiden name, and posing as a horse trader.

For some months, 'Palmer' prospered in his new trade but he was far from honest. In February 1739 he was found to have a stolen horse for sale in his yard and was arrested. Investigations began and it soon became clear to the magistrates that 'John Palmer' had appeared from nowhere. Suspecting that it was a name assumed to hide the man's real identity, the magistrates threw 'Palmer' into prison to await further investigations. 'Palmer' then wrote a letter to his brother in Essex asking him to write a letter fraudulently backing up his false identity. By sheer luck the letter was seen in the post office by John Smith, Turpin's old schoolteacher. Smith recognised the handwriting and wrote to inform the authorities in York that 'Palmer' was really Dick Turpin.

Turpin's fate was sealed, but he faced it bravely and in the style expected of a gentleman of the road. He called in a tailor to make him a new suit in which to be executed. He then sent for the landlord of a York tavern and paid in advance for a lavish party for all his friends and family to attend after the funeral. On the day of his execution, Turpin walked firmly to the scaffold. He made a speech confessing his crimes and urging young men not to follow his path to death. Then he put the noose around his neck and jumped.

Turpin's life was one of high adventure, base crimes and great excitement. But that was not enough for the public. Within a few years the forces of law and order had driven highwaymen from the roads, and Turpin turned out to have been the last of his kind to have enjoyed any real success and glamour. Soon books and pamphlets were being produced that romanticised his life, missing out the more brutal episodes, and ascribing to Turpin the feats performed by others.

Chief among these was the famous ride to York. This almost incredible feat was actually carried out in 1682 by a Yorkshire highwayman named John Nevison. This Nevison was one of those early highwaymen who had been born into the gentry, but his life of crime was prompted by lust for riches and not by unfortunate circumstances. He was unfailingly polite to ladies, often refusing to rob them of their jewels if he was flush with cash, and passed on a share of his proceeds to innkeepers and others around Pontefract to ensure their silence and support. Nevison's main business was to organise a gang of horsemen who rode the moors. They ran a protection racket on the carters who crossed the moors.

However, Nevison also liked to visit London and paid his bills on such trips by more conventional highway robbery. It was on one such trip that he stopped a coach at dawn near Rochester in Kent. His mask slipped and a man on the coach recognised him. Nevison fled and decided that his best defence would be an alibi. He decided to get as far away as possible by sunset. Putting his spurs to his horse, Nevison made for London. Changing mounts, Nevison set off up the Great North Road, now the A1. At frequent intervals he changed horses, always riding north as hard as he could. As the sun began to set he clattered in through the Micklegate Bar. Nevison then headed for the Minster and on his way passed the Lord Mayor of York, whom he knew by sight. Stopping his horse, Nevison hailed the mayor, introduced himself and asked the time. The mayor told him and then passed on.

When Nevison was arrested for the Kent robbery, he called the Lord Mayor of York as a witness to the fact that he had been in York that day. Nobody could believe that any man could ride 230 miles in a single day, so Nevison was acquitted. Like Turpin, Nevison was hanged in York after his eventual capture and trial in 1685. It seems rather unfair that popular imagination has it that the phantom highwayman of St George's Field is Turpin and not the rather more deserving and much more local Nevison.

The Grey Lady of the Foss

Ignore the bridge over the Ouse on the right, but bear left past the castle to cross the Foss. On the far side of the bridge over this stream, turn north up Piccadilly. After 150 yards this street

A ghostly grey lady stalks this bridge over the Foss that leads into Walmgate.

re-crosses the Foss. Just before the bridge turn sharp right. Where this lane ends in a T-junction, turn left into Fossgate and cross the Foss to find a shopping street that runs off toward the Minster. Here you might encounter another grey lady.

A Sense of Brooding Evil at Walmgate

Turn around to return back down Fossgate to cross stream and continue straight on. The road here is known as Walmgate. A shop that was demolished here in the 1980s had long stood empty, partly on account of the sense of brooding evil that some felt in the upstairs front room used as an office.

The Five Lions Hotel has a ghost that goes by the name of Green Jenny, though nobody knows if that is her real name.

The Mystery of Green Jenny at the Five Lions Pub

Still standing is the Five Lions pub on the left. This pub was formerly a venue for cockfighting, before that sport was outlawed. The ghost here goes by the name of Green Jenny, though nobody knows if that is her real name. She is seen most often toward the rear of the building. As her name indicates she wears a long dress of a dark green colour. So far as can be deduced from sightings, her fashions place her in the early nineteenth century. There are no stories attached to this phantom, so it is impossible to know what it is that keeps her ghost in the pub.

The Topless Ghost of the Black Swann Inn

Continue to the end of Walmgate and pass through the city walls. Turn left along Foss Islands Road, keeping the walls on your left. After once again crossing the Foss stream turn left into Peasholme Green. Here you will find the Black Swan Inn, which has a most peculiar ghost.

There is sometimes a phantom man coming down the staircase, or at least part of him. The ghost is seen only from the waist downward. He wears trousers and a pair of boots, but he makes no sound as his footwear clumps on the stairs. Since the rest of his body is never seen, the age from which he dates is quite unknown. Men's trousers and boots don't really change much in fashion over the years.

The bar of this pub has two distinct ghosts. The first and more active is the phantom of a short, plump Victorian man dressed in the plain clothes of a workman. He sports a bowler hat as he sits impatiently in a corner. The man fidgets and tuts audibly as if he is waiting for someone or something to arrive. Quite clearly it never does.

The second ghost in the bar is more serene. This takes the form of a young woman dressed in a long gown who stands by the fireplace gazing at the mantelpiece. She has long blonde hair that hangs loose over her shoulders and is reported to be remarkably pretty. When she has been seen in the evening, witnesses say that she seems to emit a slight whitish glow from all over her body.

The Black Swan Inn has a most peculiar ghost, which consists of only the bottom half of a man.

The Cinderella Ghost and the Phantom Viking at the Church of St Saviour

Continue to the end of Peasholme Green, then turn right into Spen Lane before turning left into St Saviourgate, where yet another grey lady appears. This particular ghost is rather better defined than the usual grey lady, for she wears fashions that firmly date her to the later eighteenth century and follows a set routine. On the nights she is seen, this lady appears on the stroke of midnight emerging from the Church of St Saviour which gives the road its name. She then walks along the length of the church until she reaches the far end of the building. There she waits, anxiously looking around as if expecting somebody to come to meet her. After a few seconds she vanishes. She is sometimes seen pacing up and down, still waiting, but never past 1 a.m. It would appear that her time on Earth is limited to the hour from midnight to 1 a.m.

There is a persistent tale told about the church that is impossible to verify. At some date in the early twentieth century, a man who was determined to discover where the ghostly lady began her walk asked for permission to stay in the church overnight. The vicar agreed, and at dusk the intrepid watcher was locked into the church.

Next morning the vicar returned, unlocked he door and called out to see if the man had succeeded in his quest. There was nothing but silence. The vicar called again, but again hear heard nothing. Beginning to feel worried he began searching the church. He found no sign of the man, so hurried off to summon the verger and others. The would-be ghost watcher was eventually found up in the roof, having somehow clambered up there in the night. According to one version of the tale the man was a gibbering wreck having been terrified witless by something that had happened that night. A more dramatic version has it that the man was dead from fright with an expression of utter horror on his face.

Equally difficult to pin down is a report that another ghost is to be seen just outside the church. This phantom, reports suggest, is a Viking. He wears a helmet and a shirt of iron mail while in his hand he brandishes a sword. Those who tell this tale say that the Viking was executed here for some unspecified crime in the early middle ages.

Return back along St Saviourgate to Spen Lane, then turn right. Take the first left into Aldwark. Follow Aldwark northwest to the junction with Goodramgate. Cross over Goodramgate to enter Ogleforth. This lane bends sharp left after a few yards. Follow the lane as it bends and continue on into College Street to return to the Treasurer's House.

Other titles published by The History Press

Paranormal West Yorkshire
ANDY OWENS

With famous cases such as the Cottingley Fairies, the Pontefract Poltergeist, and eyewitness accounts of ghosts, black cats and UFOs, this richly illustrated collection covers a fascinating range of strange events from West Yorkshire's history. Including sources both ancient and modern and with never-before published investigations by the Haunted Yorkshire Psychical Research Group, this book will delight all lovers of the unexplained.

978 0 7524 4810 7

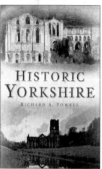

Historic Yorkshire
RICHARD A. POWELL

Including subjects as diverse as Roman Yorkshire, Yorkshire castles and abbeys, historic York and coaching days in Yorkshire, prehistoric Yorkshire, Yorkshire folklore, Robin Hood of Yorkshire, ghost houses, and industry, canals and railways, this volume is a fascinating tour through Yorkshire's past. Richly illustrated and meticulously researched, this book will delight all lovers of the Dales.

978 0 7524 4926 5

Hanged at York
STEPHEN WADE

The condemned featured here range from coiners and forgers to murderers, thieves and highwaymen, the most infamous being Dick Turpin, who was hanged on York's Knavesmire in 1739 for horse-stealing. Up to 1856, York Castle was the principal place of execution for persons convicted in all three Ridings of Yorkshire. There was also another gallows in York, at the City Gaol, and it was here that David Anderson was hanged for uttering forged banknotes in 1809. Stephen Wade's highly readable new book is fully illustrated with photographs, news cuttings and engravings.

978 0 7509 5042 8

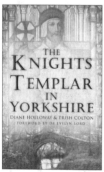

The Knights Templar in Yorkshire
DIANE HOLLOWAY & TRISH COLTON

This book explores what life was like during the Templars' stay in Yorkshire. Not only was it the biggest county in Britain, but in Templar terms it was also the richest. They owned more land, property and people in Yorkshire than in any other county in England. This volume takes the reader on an intimate tour of the ten major Templar sites established in Yorkshire, and reveals what life was like for their inhabitants, how the land was farmed, what the population ate, how they were taxed and local legends.

978 0 7509 5087 9

Visit our website and discover thousands of other History Press books.
www.thehistorypress.co.uk

The History Press